JOHN KILLINGER

The Miracle of Prayer and Meditation

Bread for the Wilderness
Wine for the Journey

WORD BOOKS
PUBLISHER
4800 WEST WACO DRIVE
WACO, TEXAS
76703

Bread for the Wilderness, Wine for the Journey
First Printing—March 1976
Second Printing—June 1976
Third Printing—February 1977
Fourth Printing—April 1978
First Paperback Printing—September 1979
Second Paperback Printing—January 1981

Quotations marked NEB are from *The New English Bible* © The Delegates of The Oxford University Press and The Syndics of The Cambridge University Press, 1961, 1970, and are used by permission.

Quotations marked RSV are from The Revised Standard Version, copyrighted 1946 (renewed 1973), 1956, and © 1971 by the Division of Christian Education of the National Council of the Churches of Christ in the U.S.A., and are used by permission.

ISBN 0-8499-2896-6
Library of Congress catalog card number: 75-38049

The Miracle of Prayer and Meditation

*With special gratitude to
Miss Lillian Vaughn
who encouraged us to pray.*

Contents

Don Juan had once told me that a man of knowledge had predilections. I asked him to explain his statement.

"My predilection is to see," he said.

"What do you mean by that?"

"I like to see," he said, "because only by seeing can a man of knowledge know."

"What kind of things do you see?"

"Everything."

"But I also see everything and I'm not a man of knowledge."

"No. You don't see."

"I think I do."

"I tell you, you don't."

"What makes you say that, don Juan?"

"You only look at the surface of things."

—Carlos Castaneda, A Separate Reality

1
Prayer

and the Wilderness

Life can be a wilderness or a paradise. It all depends upon how you look at it and what you make of it.

If it has seemed like a wilderness to you, that's because you have seen it as a wilderness. Some people, given the same life and the same opportunities, would have seen it differently. They would have thanked God for the paradise.

It's the point of view—of how you see things.

There's a little verse I heard as a boy that expresses it:

> Two men looked out
> From prison bars:
> One saw the mud,
> The other saw the stars.

Even people who have borne great tragedy have viewed the world with courage and optimism.

One lovely woman I know was told by her doctor that she had an incurable disease. "Then I shall live a lifetime every day," she said.

I met a couple who were parents of a retarded son. They loved him with that special tenderness his condition required. When he died at seventeen, still with the mind of an infant, they held him in their arms and gave thanks to God for all he had meant to them during those difficult years.

A man born without arms learned to dress and feed himself with his feet. His "handwriting" was beautiful, accomplished with a pencil held in his teeth. He earned a living and lived normally in almost every way.

"Nothing is a handicap," he said, "until you begin to think of it as a handicap."

That is precisely the handicap most of us live with: we *think* we are handicapped. We see the world as a wilderness and not as a paradise. We behold the mud instead of the stars. Or, in religious terms, we experience the absence of God instead of his presence.

A lot has been said in recent years about the absence of God, as though it were a fact confirmed by all the evidence of modern life. Some people have spoken of it almost elatedly, as if the idea of a divine presence were some unbearable weight lifted at last from humanity's shoulders.

Perhaps the idea is in itself an unbearable weight. But I wonder how many of those persons have ever really experienced the presence of God. If you have, you know how ludicrous such talk of his absence really is.

There is never a moment when he could be more present.

The problem is with us. We lose the ability to

discern his presence. We forget how to pray. The paradise reverts to wilderness.

How to see again! That is what we want. How to live every day as though the world were paradise and not wilderness, as though all of life were filled with the miracles of God!

That is what we desire more than anything else—to see the miracles again!

Well, you can. You really can!

All you have to do is learn to pray. It's that simple. Prayer develops a whole new consciousness, a whole new way of looking at the world. By putting you in touch with God, amid your very circumstances, it enables you to see the paradise around you.

I know, because I am beginning to see it again.

There was a time when I saw it very clearly. It was during my adolescence. I lived, like young Wordsworth, with "intimations of immortality" all around me. I lived, breathed, slept with a sense of the presence of God. Every bush was a burning bush, every creek a sacred stream.

Once I saw an angel, bright as the sun, diaphanous as a movie projection. There was no question of its reality. I had not yet fallen into the way of dividing objective and subjective phenomena which our educational system teaches and enforces in us. The vision was a gift, as life itself was. I saw with a single eye.

Then the world began to wean me away from belief in angels. Not suddenly or dramatically, but gradually. I became caught up in its frantic pace. I learned to speak the language of its jaunty secularism and self-assurance. I submitted to its subtle way of psychologizing everything about me—my dreams, my loves, even my beliefs.

The enthusiasm, the fire that had burned inside me, was artfully damped. The living flame became a hidden coal.

I have warmed myself at that coal for years. It has kept me going through college and seminary, marriage, career, parenthood.

Now I want it to flame out again, to burn freely, wildly, and joyously the way it once did. I want it to consume me again. And there are signs that it is going to. Little clues. Small indications.

So many things have begun to converge—what I know, what I feel, what I have experienced.

Perhaps if I share these with you, you will recognize them in your own life, and the gift of prayer will visit you again as it is visiting me.

The main thing is the way the clues have begun to fit together to dispel the pseudo-scientific impression I have had for so long that the universe is highly mechanistic and predetermined, impervious to human or divine will.

What a devil's ruse that is! It deterred me more than anything else from following my earliest inclinations toward a life of prayer and holiness. Not that I suddenly stopped believing. No, it wasn't like that. Instead, it was slow, deteriorative, corrosive.

"What is the use of praying?" a voice in my heart quietly insinuated. "How can it possibly do any good?"

Oh, I knew that prayer conditions the self, always disposing it to an easier acceptance of life's angularities. But what is that compared with the wonderful view of prayer in the Bible or among the great medieval mystics? Such a view seemed cold, depressive, unfaithful.

But somewhere along the way, after several years of slipping downhill in my attempts to pray, I began to see that life—the world, the big picture—is not so rationally determined as I had been led to believe. The order is less orderly, the rules are less regular, the certainty is less certain. Mystery is the true order of things. A *wildness* lies in wait, as G. K. Chesterton once said. Our mathematics was not wrong, but too small. Truth is not necessarily *other* than what modern man has discovered, but it is *more* than he has discovered.

Strange as it may seem, I began to come to this insight while working in the Theater of the Absurd. Looking back, I realize it was a miracle. God used those often agnostic, despairing spirits to speak to my own weak faith and troubled soul.

I was in Paris, writing *World in Collapse: The Vision of Absurd Drama.* As a background for understanding the writers of the absurd, I was studying the annals of the Dadaists and surrealists, their zany, irrepressible forebears. Duchamp, who mocked the great traditions of art; Robert Desnos, who spoke poetry in a trance; Apollinaire, who stood drama on its ear. At first, I confess, they seemed mere pranksters—ingenious publicists who always managed to get photographed throwing dead cats into cathedrals. But gradually their flamboyant opposition to rationalism insinuated itself upon me for the deeper philosophy it is.

The world, I realized, *is* less orderly than our traditions deceive us into believing. Our perceptions of what is real do become fixed and habitual, so that knowing takes the place of experiencing. The patterns must be broken sometimes to remind us of this.

I remember the precise occasion on which these

truths became inner revelations to me.

It was a Sunday afternoon and I had gone to the little Theatre Rochechouart to see a performance of Arrabal's *Le Cimetière des voitures,* "The Car Cemetery." It was a fabulous production—surrealistic, unpredictable, cacophonous. The characters lived in the battered hulks of old automobiles strewn over the stage and suspended above it. Lights flashed erratically at the spectators as well as at the actors. Stage aprons had been constructed around the entire wall, and the action took place everywhere at once, with the audience trying to follow it in revolving chairs. Sirens wailed, chains were struck against sheets of metal, the actors stamped, screamed, cried, ranted.

After nearly three hours, I dazedly stumbled back into the quiet back streets of Paris. It was as though I had entered a dream! The world inside, harsh and improbable as it was, had become my reality, and now the world outside seemed artificial and repellent. I wanted to rush back inside at once.

I cannot fully describe the impact this experience had on me. Suddenly I knew, with my whole being, what all the great philosophers from Plato to McLuhan have tried to say to us: that our views of life and the world are shaped by what we are taught and accept, and that once we have accepted these views and ceased to challenge them, life shrinks to their proportions. It was a horrifying realization! Had my life diminished to the size of my rational conception of the world? I hoped not, but I feared the worst.

Where could I go to learn more about perception and reality? From the Theater of the Absurd, I turned to Zen Buddhism. I read Watts, Suzuki, Dumoulin, Kapleau, and other interpreters of the Zen experience.

I was fascinated! Here was an entire philosophy of life, almost a religion, devoted to breaking the usual circuits of logic and getting beyond a merely rational approach to existence. Some Zen Buddhists sat for years contemplating emptiness or meditating on *koans* such as "What is the sound of one hand clapping?" all in order to transcend the systems of reason and arrive at a more intuitive, mystical grasp of life.

I traveled to Kyoto and sat for hours staring at the famous rock garden of Ruonji, which some authorities think is the consummate expression of Zen art. I listened to the musical trickling of water from the bamboo pipes of Zen drinking fountains. I strolled through the woods at the Temple of the Silver Pavilion, photographing the blotches of snow which fell silently through the dense pine foliage onto the moss below. I absorbed the culture the way a hungry man revels in food. It seemed to speak of eternity in the midst of a teeming, chaotic world.

From Zen, I turned to Thomas Merton, whom I had read years ago, and to the Trappist experience of silence. Merton had been "into" Zen, and had in fact died in Bangkok. What did the silence have to do with all of it? Merton said in his *Secular Journal* that the first time he left the monastery at Gethsemani to go into Louisville, the nearest city, the noises were so palpable as to seem nearly unbearable to him. He realized that the little Trappist community where people spoke only to God was the linchpin holding the entire world together!

Were prayer and Zen related? Prayer and surrealism? Prayer and absurdity?

Eagerly I devoured William Johnston's *The Still Point*, which explored the relationship between Zen and medieval western mysticism. And then I read his *Christian Zen,* which was briefer but far more personal. Father Johnston, a Jesuit, had taught at Tokyo's Sophia University for more than twenty years. He saw extended similarities between Zen meditation and Christian prayer, especially as the latter is practiced in retreats and monasteries where the discipline is stricter than when individuals attempt to pray alone.

I was hooked! Eventually, I knew, I had to write a book on prayer, if for no other reason than to sort out my own feelings and beliefs on the subject.

I began to talk with other Christians to learn what their experience of prayer had been. Some of what I heard made the hair on my neck stand on end!

One woman, whose name is Olive, told me about the time her father had a heart attack. He was very near the front door when it happened and his wife, who was alone with him in the house, caught him as he began to fall. The poor woman lacked the strength either to lay him down on the floor or to get him to a sofa. She didn't know what to do. All she could do was support him where she had him.

She was a very religious woman but she had never believed in asking God for special favors. Now, however, in the exigency of the moment, she implored him for help.

Presently there was a knock at the door. "Come in!" she cried, "Come in!" The door opened and a strange man walked in. Seeing the situation and the woman's great distress, he quickly assisted her in getting her husband to the bed and summoning a doctor.

"I don't know what came over me," the man said afterwards. "I never come this way to town. But today, as I approached the intersection, I experienced an irresistible urge to take this street. And then, as I was passing your house, the same feeling caused me to turn in and knock at your door. I don't know what possessed me!"

What does one do with such "miracle" stories as this? Dismiss them? Bracket them, and set them aside from the context of everyday life, so that they do not have to be dealt with?

I confess that is what I would once have done with them. They do seem to be interruptions in the normal pattern of experience, surds, irreducible cinders in the grater of reason.

But what if the interruptions are there to save us from the normal pattern? What if they point us to new ways of looking at life which, taken as the whole, are no less reasonable than our present ways of looking at it, but are only larger and more comprehensive?

This is precisely the attitude many scientists have assumed toward reports of extrasensory perception (ESP) and psychokinesis (PK)—persons' ability to foretell events, communicate through barriers or over great distances, and influence the behavior of physical objects by concentrating on them. As Dr. J. B. Rhine of Duke University said in *The Reaches of the Mind*, the quantity or regularity of the occurrences is not the determining factor in establishing the truth of their existence. Several of our known energies appeared to observers first as the faintest of manifestations— mere sparks. As a matter of fact, said Dr. Rhine, almost all discoveries in nuclear physics, chemistry, and the biology of heredity are inferences made from apparently random and insignificant data. The important thing is not to dismiss the data before one's scientific philosophy is large enough to accommodate them.*

How little we really know about the universe we inhabit! How poorly we have decoded the messages of existence, especially when they have come from sources we did not consider scientifically respectable. Now, as I enter the second half of my life, I am trying to be open again, the way I was as a child. I am fascinated by ESP, PK, biofeedback, and altered states of consciousness (ASC). The world is indeed a more complex thing than Newtonian physics suspected. The mind and emotions interact with matter in ways early scientists never guessed.

Take the simple experiment which Dr. Rhine and his associates at Duke University performed with dice. They found that some persons, by concentrating on dice thrown either by hand or from mechanical projectors, can cause certain numbers on the face of the dice to appear with extraordinary frequency. They also found that on second or third sets of rolls, the average number of "hits" by the same person declines, indicating that the person's power of concentration is stronger at first and then diminishes.

This evidence of telepathic power, produced in a laboratory under the watchful eye of university scien-

---

*Cf. this statement by Lawrence LeShan in *The Medium, the Mystic, and the Physicist:* "If we have learned one thing from science, it is that the atypical case, the unusual incident, is the one that—if looked at seriously—teaches us about all the others. It is the one substance in Madame Curie's workshop that glows in the dark that teaches us about the basic structure of all the others. It is the one Petri dish in Fleming's laboratory in which the germs die unexpectedly that leads us to the discovery of the antibiotics. It is the one set of flasks in Pasteur's experiments in which life does *not* appear that teaches us the source of life in the others. It is the atypical paralysis in which neurology can *not* find the lesion that leads Freud to the discovery of the unconscious. It is the one problem in physics (the addition of velocities problem) that cannot be solved in the usual way that leads to an Einsteinian revolution and gives us a deeper understanding of the problems we had been able to solve in the old way."

tists, has had an indescribable impact on my scientific world-view. For years I had trouble believing in intercessory prayer because it seemed to contradict what I had been taught about the inexorable laws of physical matter. Now I learn that there is no conflict at all, that there are no inexorable laws, and that mind and matter interact on each other all the time.

The most obvious locus of this interaction, of course, is in our own bodies. For a long time there have been people who believed that the mind had almost unlimited power to heal the body or keep it well, if only a person knew how to unleash that power. A friend of mine who is a Christian Scientist says that he has been ill only rarely in his life, and then only at periods when his mind was depressed or lacking in faith. During the Second World War, he said, he often slept in foxholes, cold and wet to the skin, without suffering so much as a case of sniffles.

Is it possible that despite discoveries
and progress, despite culture,
religion and world-wisdom, one has remained
on the surface of life?

—Rainer Maria Rilke
The Notebooks
of Malte Laurids Brigge

As I talked with people about prayer, I began to hear more and more stories of miraculous recoveries from physical injury or disease. A woman in Louisiana came up to me after a lecture and told me that she was five years old. "In my second life, that is," she explained. Five and a half years ago the doctors had told her she had incurable cancer in the lungs and breast. It had spread too widely to be operable. They said she had six months to live.

"I was ready to give up," she said. "But my daughter wasn't. She belonged to a charismatic prayer group. She and her husband literally dragged me to it one night. I didn't want to go but they insisted. 'Mama, you don't have to do anything but come,' my daughter said. They wouldn't take no for an answer, so I went."

Everyone in the group laid hands on her and prayed for her. "It was the strangest feeling," she said. "All those people touching me and praying for me. I didn't know what to think. It excited me. I felt something—like power—going into me. Afterwards, I didn't feel it so much, but there was still a tingle of it that didn't go away."

When the woman began to feel better instead of worse, the doctors gave her additional tests. "They were amazed," she said. "Not a single sign of cancer. It had all gone away. I figured my life had started over again. So now I'm five years old."

Two of her children and her son-in-law stood by her side, beaming.

"And the important thing is," she added, "that I'm *really* alive now. Life is more spiritual. I'm excited about everything!"

Excited about everything. That's perhaps the best description of how I began to feel as I saw the walls dropping between all of these heretofore separated areas of life and thought—surrealism, Zen meditation, ESP, PK, mind-body interaction. Man is a wall-building creature, I thought. What if God is trying to get us to tear them down and start over again?

For a while I became very interested in drugs and their potential for raising or lowering human consciousness. I didn't take drugs myself, but I never tired of reading or hearing the reports of those who did. I had avidly studied Aldous Huxley's *The Doors of Perception,* in which he described his own experiences with hallucinogens, and I knew that many of the brilliant works by such writers as Tom Wolfe, Ken Kesey, and Richard Brautigan were the result of consciousness-raising trips on LSD and marijuana.

I spent an entire evening talking with two homosexuals, an actor and an off-Broadway playwright about their drug experiences. The playwright described one experience at great length. He was lying on his bed in a darkened room. As the drug took effect, his friend, who was acting as his "guide" on the trip, lit a candle on the table and put a Szymanowski recording on the turntable.

"The candlelight seemed to rise and fall with the music," he said. "It would seem to swell and swell until it filled the room, and then it would die down to nothing. It seemed to be inside my body, not just in the room itself. I felt the music as if it were a symphony in my very being, as if I were a cathedral and it were filling me in every part. And the light—the light would fill me too, then it would go away.

"When it went away, I would begin to cry. I couldn't stand it. Then it would return again, and I would laugh with joy.

"Afterwards," he said, "when I went out into the street, everything seemed more alive. I saw the very bricks of the buildings. *Saw* them, I tell you. How many times had I looked at those buildings and not seen the bricks? But now I saw them, each one of them, and wanted to touch them and feel them. Everything was so vivid, it was almost painful."

How was this related to religious experience, I wondered. It sounded like passages from the mystics about ecstatic moments and how they made the world more bright and beautiful. My own attempts at praying, especially during adolescence, had frequently been accompanied by similar feelings. Were drugs really necessary to alter consciousness?

Then I discovered John Lilly, the fascinating psychoanalyst and biophysicist. For years, Lilly worked at the problem of communicating with dolphins. He spent literally days at a time in a wetsuit, lying in a tank with the dolphins, so that they would be familiar with him and pursue their normal routines of relationship with each other as if he were not there.

One night, said Lilly, lying there in the dark tank he began to feel communication from a distant star. It had been proven, he knew, that ESP is not affected at all by time or space. Suppose some being on another planet was sending a message to him, and he had received it because he was lying there so openly and patiently in such a receptive mood.

The thought galvanized him. There are no limits, he saw, to the reach of the mind—only such arbitrary limits as we are willing to impose.

It was the beginning of a pilgrimage for Lilly. It took him to South America, where he sat for months in a cave in the mountains, learning meditation from an old man reputed to have great powers. He went into drugs to explore their psychedelic qualities. Then he went to California, to Esalen and La Jolla, to see what he could learn from the interdisciplinary studies of mind and body there. He is convinced, he says, that we have only begun to realize the extent to which our minds and bodies are interrelated, and to which our minds can travel freely through the universe, even "visiting" with people in other countries or on other planets.

Without awareness there is nothing.

—Fritz Perls
In and Out of the Garbage Pail

During this same period of growth and reevaluation in my life, I was teaching a Sunday seminar on death in a local Presbyterian church. As one thing generally leads to another, so it did on the question of consciousness. I began to realize that we would not have dealt fully with the topic of death until we had considered some of the vast array of literature on personal survival beyond death.

I did not realize how vast the array was until one day I stepped into a little university bookstore specializing in books on the occult and mystical. There were shelves and shelves of such books, running to perhaps thirty or forty feet in length! Obviously I had been living in an intellectual ghetto, not to realize what popular interest there is in such matters.

The one book that continues to intrigue me, of the many I either read or perused on the subject, is Bishop Pike's *The Other Side*. This book relates the bishop's attempts, several times successful, to get in touch with his son who had died bizarrely a few months earlier. I suppose my fascination with this particular book is due in large measure to the respect I had entertained for the bishop himself. Trained as a lawyer, he had entered the ministry late, but had then shown such competency, both as a preacher and as an administrator, that he had been elevated to the episcopacy. And what I admired about him more than anything else, I think, was his tough-mindedness as a theologue and catalyst. He was a no-nonsense cleric, dismissing unintelligible old dogmas and fussy ecclesiastical habits with a cavalierness that kept him in constant hot water with the college of bishops.

"Jim Pike has flipped," they all exclaimed when he began speaking of attending séances, consorting with mediums, and communicating with his dead son.

But I wasn't so sure. The very unlikeliness of such behavior in Pike seemed to impart credibility to it. And I was especially captivated by a Schiller quotation he had included in *The Other Side.* It said: "Single facts can never be 'proved' except by their coherence in a system. But, as all facts come singly, anyone who dismisses them one by one is destroying the conditions under which the conviction of new truth could arise in his mind."

It is important to be open, to hold the evidence in abeyance.

In our death seminar, we also discussed the writings of people who argue the case for reincarnation after death or transmigration of the soul. Among these were certain books and pamphlets of Dr. Leslie Weatherhead, the eminent and widely respected minister of City Temple in London, who was such a comfort and inspiration to thousands of people during the terrible period of incendiary bombing in that city.

One night as the seminar continued, I had a remarkably vivid dream in which I seemed to experience previous incarnations of my own spirit. First I was conscious of rising to the surface of a murky, slime-flecked pool as a turtle. Then I found myself in the role of Genghis Khan, galloping on a horse pell-mell across some Oriental terrain, brandishing a sword or scimitar as I rode. And finally I dreamed of myself as a medieval monk, sitting quietly in a small cell copying manuscripts.

When I told my wife the next day of the powerful effect I felt from the dream, she exclaimed, "Well, you should have, because you are all three of them!"

She was right. There are times when I feel like the primeval turtle, peering out from a wonderful shell at the world taking place around me. Then there are times when I come on like a thundering Mongol, thirsty for excitement and conquest, full of confidence in myself to accomplish whatever I set out to accomplish. And of course I spend many hours like a monk, pecking away at my typewriter, loving the solitude, the words, and what they create on paper.

Sometime later, my maiden aunt died in Iowa. She was a strong pioneer woman, the proud daughter of an immigrant who had been a western lawman and a leading farmer in his part of the country. Although I had visited her relatively few times in my life, I always retained a very vivid image of her stoutness, her blazing eyes, and her wonderful, dominating voice. She and I had always communicated easily.

A few nights before she died suddenly and unexpectedly, I had dreamed of her, and had some foreboding premonition about her. I told this to my wife. When the news of her death reached us, our phone was out of order and a neighbor came to the door to ask us to call my parents, to whom we had given the neighbor's number. At the moment he knocked on the door, Anne was leafing through a cookbook which my aunt had given her several years before. It was the first time she had picked up the book in months.

Anne and I both felt strange for several days, as though my aunt were somehow present to us in a way she had never been in life. Then, several weeks later, I was sitting on our bedroom patio reading a book. It was a warm, pleasant day, and a little fountain was bubbling and gurgling at one end of the patio. Suddenly I felt my aunt's presence and looked up. A small butterfly circled the fountain. It flew nearer and landed on a stump which held a flower pot. It seemed to be regarding me with almost human vision. Then it flew directly to me and lit on my hand. Something electric went through me! I knew it was my aunt.

Several times in subsequent days I saw the same butterfly hovering about the patio, and each time I experienced the same intimations. I laughed at the irony of it. My aunt was such a large woman, and the butterfly was so small and fragile. But it seemed somehow appropriate that a person who had had to lumber through life as an overweight farmwoman should be reincarnated as a sylphlike moth.

Certain instincts now caution me to withdraw from such confessions, for I know with what disdain they are likely to be greeted in a world dominated by reason and sobriety of thought. My colleagues in the theological seminary will cluck their tongues and say that their worst suspicions are now confirmed.

But I am trying to suggest something of what has been happening in my mind over the past few years to bring me to where I am in my present inquiry into the nature and meaning of prayer. For I feel of a certainty it is all related, even though plausible psychological explanations might be suggested for some of the phenomena I have reported, such as Lilly's reception of alien messages, Bishop Pike's "visits" with his son, my own dreams of reincarnation, and my impression of my dead aunt's presence.

The relationship lies somehow in the deeper nature of the mind and its ability to transcend the barriers of torpor and incredulity imposed on it by habits of thinking now being exposed in numerous ways as grossly inadequate. We may be forced to take leave of our senses, as our present empiricist world-view might regard it, in order to find them and pay attention to them again. We have tended for too long to suppress our belief in any occurrences or phenomena which do not fit easily within the molds of our scientific prejudices.

Unless we are willing to entertain the possibility of their truthfulness, coming to us as they do, one by one, then we cannot ever, as Schiller suggested, approach any significant new configurations of truth and factuality. We destroy the various pieces of evidence before they have a chance to become whole.

I have found in recent years that I am a much more belief-ful person than I thought I was, and I suspect that you might find the same about yourself. Our capacity to enter into strange reports, and to attribute a measure of reality to them, is not only greater than most of us suppose, but actually increases to the degree that it is exercised.

What is more, our lives become more exciting as our believing faculties are enlarged. They engage in hope again. Not just an eschatological possibility awaiting the vague apocalyptic future and its infinite potential, but hope as a daily event belonging to exist- ence here and now because it is predicated on a present openness, because our lives are no longer closed systems or foregone conclusions.

This is why I think that prayer—opening ourselves to God and the many ways he has of speaking to us—is not just a part of the Christian life, but *is* the Christian life.

It is only as we learn to pray that the meaning of faith comes alive to us, and that the presence of God in Christ becomes real to us. Until then, all of the dogmas and teachings of the early church are only stumbling blocks to our understanding, for they, like prayer itself, seem to fly in the face of all that we have agreed to know about ourselves and our world.

Until then, the world remains a wilderness.

The mockingbird took a single step into the air and dropped. His wings were still folded against his sides as though he were singing from a limb and not falling, accelerating thirty-two feet per second per second, through empty air. Just a breath before he would have been dashed to the ground, he unfurled his wings with exact, deliberate care, revealing the broad bars of white, spread his elegant, white-banded tail, and so floated onto the grass. I had just rounded a corner when his insouciant step caught my eye; there was no one else in sight. The fact of his free fall was like the old philosophical conundrum about the tree that falls in the forest. The answer must be, I think, that beauty and grace are performed whether or not we will or sense them. The least we can do is try to be there.

—*Annie Dillard,* Pilgrim at Tinker Creek

2

Prayer

and the Kingdom

The world is full of miracles that most of us never see. We have not trained ourselves to look. We are like processionary caterpillars, those pathetic insects which, if led onto the lip of a fruitjar, will join ranks head-to-tail and proceed around the jar until they fall starving and exhausted to the ground. Blindly we make our way from the cradle to the grave.

Maybe not from the cradle. Babies probably see more than adults. The world is mystery to them. They want to taste, touch, fondle everything, because they are filled with wonder.

But when we become familiar with our habitat, we cease to wonder. We accept the presence of things without marveling at them, as though they were not miracles.

This makes a great difference in how we pray. If we live as drudges, content only to acquire a little property and make it from day to day, seeing no miracles, then we will pray for miracles.

Not the right kind of miracles, of course. But miracles such as a winning sweepstakes ticket, a chance at a better job, relief from a nagging backache, or a love affair with an enchanting stranger. Miracles which, nine times out of ten, would leave us poorer than we were.

It is on the basis of miracles like these that prayer gets a bad name.

It is when we see the world for what it is, a miracle in itself—a miracle filled with miracles—that prayer comes into its own. Then prayer reaches its highest nature, its finest meaning, as gratitude.

Then we are thankful for what is, rather than what is not. We see that the creation is good. *Tūv, tūv,* as the Bible says, lacking adverbial modifiers—"good, good," or very good. There is too much to be thankful for to worry about what we don't have.

"When we were young," says Father Evely, "we learned that there were four types of prayer: adoration, thanksgiving, petition and repentance. But for me now there is only one: the Eucharist."

Eucharist—thanksgiving—the Mass, in which we go to church to hear again, in the Word, what God has given us, and to eat again, in the bread and wine, what he has provided.

Evely is right, you know: we do not go to church to serve God. That is a pagan notion. Our deity does not have to be placated. We do not have to cajole him into being bounteous to us. He is already bounteous. We go to be served, to have him put on the apron and spread a table before us. We go to be sensitized to what he has already given.

That is the point of the gospel, isn't it? Jesus said:

The spirit of the Lord is upon me because
  he has anointed me;
he has sent me to announce good news to the poor,
to proclaim release for prisoners and recovery
  of sight for the blind;
to let the broken victims go free,
to proclaim the year of the Lord's favour.

Luke 4:18-19, NEB

Good news to those who can't pay. The world is free. Life is a gift. It is all a miracle.

How did Jesus know this?

It came to him through days and nights of listening to God, of waiting for what God had to say to him, of tuning his inner ear to catch the slightest whisper.

For forty days—more than a month—he was alone in the wilderness, among the little creatures of the rocks, learning what makes a paradise of desert places. And when he knew, he began his ministry.

"The Kingdom of God," he said, "is within you."

It was a startling announcement, and a heretical one! Few believed it. Especially those who had been working hardest to find the kingdom outside themselves.

We see some of them as Jesus encountered them or spoke about them:

A young ruler who prided himself on the punctiliousness with which he had observed the commandments in the Torah, but couldn't accept the simple, open faith of Jesus because it would mean letting go his great wealth.

A property-owner who had a year of bumper crops, but died on the eve of letting his contracts for new storage bins—possibly from the strain of management.

A fellow who went bankrupt putting his money out to usury, and then, forgiven his prison sentence by a considerate judge, went out and raised Cain against one of his own mortgagees.

A priest and temple-keeper so intent upon their religious duties that they would not stop to help a poor wayfarer who had been robbed and wounded along the road.

Pious people standing on the street corners wailing out long prayers of contrition, as though God were a long way off and would hear them for their much speaking.

Over and over, the same story. They were all too busy to see the miracles, too intent on finding the kingdom to realize it had come, like a thief in the night.

While we are on the subject, it should be noted that Jesus never approved of long prayers. Long *praying* was a different story. But long prayers, he said, were a waste.

His own model prayer, which he gave to the disciples and which was afterwards called the Lord's Prayer, was remarkably brief. Only fifty-seven words in *The New English Bible.* Fewer than in most telephone conversations or TV advertisements! Yet there is nothing, no human problem, no spiritual need, it does not touch upon.

Its secret, of course, is its focus on the kingdom. "Thy kingdom come." Everything else is ancillary to that.

If the one praying is aware of the kingdom, nothing

else matters. The world is miracle. God is to be adored. All grudges are dismissed. There is no need for great wealth or storage bins crammed with grain. Today's bread is enough. Life is a gift.

"Do not ask anxiously," Jesus taught the disciples, " 'What are we to eat? What are we to drink? What shall we wear?' All these are things for the heathen to run after, not for you, because your heavenly Father knows that you need them all. Set your mind on God's kingdom and his justice before everything else, and all the rest will come to you as well" (Matt. 6:31–33, NEB).

Doesn't a father know what his children need? asked Jesus. If they need bread, will he give them a stone? If they are hungry for fish, will he give them a snake?

"If you, then, bad as you are, know how to give your children what is good for them, how much more will your heavenly Father give good things to those who ask him!" (Matt. 7:11, NEB).

To make too much of the asking produces anxiety in us. It is true that Jesus said, "Ask, and you will receive" (Matt. 7:7, NEB). But that is not an invitation to perform magical acts. It is simply to be set over beside the fact that the heavenly Parent provides for us so abundantly.

It is the same graciousness I have experienced in spending the night at the home of friends. They receive me into their lovely house, which the wife has labored all day to clean for my arrival. They usher me into the most comfortable bedroom, where their own clothes have been removed from the closet to make room for mine. They set before me a sumptuous meal, served on their finest china and with their best silver. They give me an evening of devoted attention before a roaring fire in the sanctity of their family parlor. And then, when it is time to bid good night and retire to our beds, they say, "Now if you need anything, just ask."

What could I possibly need? Some toothpaste, perhaps? A paper handkerchief? A call in the morning? Trifles, all! Bagatelles. Mere nothings. Of course I shall have what I need. What is that, compared with what they have already given?

The secret is not in the length of the prayer, but in the quality of the praying. And the secret of that, in Jesus' case, lay in his days and nights of meditation, when he learned to see the world as miracle.

We know next to nothing of what he said then. Probably he said very little. The purely epigrammatic quality of his sayings would indicate that they are the clear distillations of long hours of passivity, when the mind was still and untroubled.

Eastern religions, of which Christianity was one, know much more of such things than we hyperactive westerners do. A Zen Buddhist of the Soto sect will sit for years learning to achieve perfect equanimity in the mind. Dogen, a famous master, called such meditation "the gateway to total liberation." It is said that a disciple trained for years in this art can breathe directly upon a mirror without fogging it.

We have been too busy trying to bring in the kingdom by main force and ingenuity. Now, because of what we have learned from biofeedback techniques, we are beginning to respect the power of meditation. Through EEGs, or the monitoring of the brain's electro-waves, we know that accomplished meditationists actually control the physical states of their bodies in ways we cannot. Some persons can stop their hearts from beating for considerable periods of time, from 10 to 30 seconds.

Dr. Elmer Green of the Menninger Foundation in Topeka has painstakingly recorded the ability of a yogi named Swami Rama to perform another incredible feat. Without moving a muscle, Swami Rama can consciously force the temperature in the palm of one hand to vary as much as 10 degrees within a distance of less than two inches.

We now know that there are two hemispheres in the brain, and that the left hemisphere, which controls the right hand, is the seat of the body's activism; while the right hemisphere, which controls the left hand, is given to dreaming, relaxation, and meditation. Research has shown that people who operate predominantly out of the left part of the brain are energetic, almost hyperactive people, while people who can operate out of the right side are calm and relaxed.

The evidence also indicates that left-minded persons are nonvisualizers, while their calm opposites are generally visualizers. It is the right-minded persons, in other words, who actually design the world which the activistic persons build. They are the artists, the dreamers, the religious visionaries.

What if those of us who are fretful, anxious, and success-motivated were to learn to use the other side of the brain more effectively? This is precisely what biofeedback training accomplishes. One of the delightful discoveries of the scientists is that persons who are wired up to see their own EEGs, monitoring their alpha-waves, learn almost instantly to control their waves, and so to use brain cells which before went unemployed.

In the very near future, it is predicted we shall all be able to use biofeedback to inspect our internal workings on a regular basis. Not only shall we be able to detect forewarnings of illness or emotional disturbance. We shall even be able to learn to live more colorful, abundant lives!

Now back to "The kingdom is within you."

The picture of Jesus we have from the Gospels is of a man who constantly alternated between retreats for prayer and highly charged interaction in the marketplace.

We do not know how he meditated when he went apart from the others. Perhaps he thought a lot about the law, for the very first words of the Psalms are:

Blessed is the man
   who walks not in the counsel of the wicked,
nor stands in the way of sinners,
   nor sits in the seat of scoffers;
but his delight is in the law of the Lord,
   and on his law he meditates day and night.
Psalm 1:1-2, RSV

This would account for Jesus' saying he came to fulfill the law, not to abolish it. Meditating on it, he would have understood that law is grace, not judgment, to those who see the kingdom of God everywhere.

But, whatever the content of his praying when he drew aside, we see the portrait of a man who thought and acted as a whole person because of his time of meditation. Never, in the record of his entire ministry, is there a sign of anxiety about whether he would have everything he needed.

Jesus was the eucharistic man, the man of thanks. He blessed the food he ate, the wine he drank, and the world he saw, because they were all gifts from his heavenly Father. He lived freely, openly, without fear. He did not grasp at life, but allowed life to come to him in its own measure, for he knew that the Father cared for him.

If we live thankfully, he showed us, a few loaves and fishes become enough to feed a multitude, and there is no agitating concern about how we shall be fed or clothed tomorrow.

Whatever Jesus asked became his. Not because he had magical powers to ask for anything and get it, but because in his joyful sense of abundance he asked only what the Father was going to give him anyway. He had an eye for the high tides of God—for what he called the kingdom—and he rode them like a surfer!

Read the Gospel of Mark if you want a good account of this. It concentrates especially on the signs of great power which accompanied the announcement of the kingdom's presence. Everywhere Jesus went, he was able to touch people and heal them or raise them from the dead. The devils, recognizing him as God's anointed, cringed before him and begged him to leave them alone.

In our limited, magical view of prayer, we are prone to imagine that Jesus was able to do these mighty works by praying and asking God for the power to do them.

But not so! A careful reading of the Gospel reveals a striking absence of references to prayer in almost all of the miracle stories. In the raising of Simon's mother (Mark 1:31), the curing of the leper (1:41), the healing of the man brought on a stretcher (2:5), the restoring of a man with a withered arm (3:5), the calming of the sea (4:39), the healing of the woman with a hemorrhage (5:29), the raising of Jairus' daughter (5:41), the curing of the Syrophoenician girl (7:29), the restoring of a blind man's sight (8:22–26), the calming of a deranged child (9:26–27), and the restoration of Bartimaeus' sight (10:52), there is not a single word about prayer! Jesus simply performed the miraculous deeds and moved on.

I do not wish to dwell too long on this matter, but I think it is important if we are to understand that the real power of prayer in Jesus' life came not from specific instances when he made requests for miracles, but from his whole life of meditation.

There are in Mark two curious references to prayer which might prove illuminating.

First, in Mark 9:14–29, is the story of the disciples' failure to cast a demon out of a boy. Jesus succeeded where they had failed. Afterwards, the disciples privately inquired, "Why could not we cast it out?"

"There is no means of casting out this sort," Jesus replied, "but prayer."

The puzzling thing is, there is no reference to Jesus' having said even the suggestion of a prayer during the exorcism. We can only conclude that he was saying to the disciples, "Only by living in an attitude of prayer can you touch the power required to do acts of this sort."

The second reference to prayer, in Mark 11:20–24, follows Jesus' cursing of the fig tree which put out leaves but held no fruit. As the little band was passing the tree on the way back to Bethany, Peter observed that the tree had withered since morning, when Jesus placed the curse on it.

Jesus' reply appears to be an out-and-out expression of the magical view of prayer: "Have faith in God.

I tell you this: if anyone says to this mountain, 'Be lifted from your place and hurled into the sea,' and has no inward doubts, but believes that what he says is happening, it will be done for him. I tell you, then, whatever you ask for in prayer, believe that you have received it and it will be yours" (Mark 11:22-24, NEB).

But we are puzzled by this, because it appears inconsistent with the other passages on prayer in Mark. So we turn to Matthew and Luke to see what those Gospels recorded about the same saying of Jesus.

Matthew reports Jesus to have remarked, "Whatever you pray for in faith you will receive" (21:22, NEB). Luke says that he said, "If you had faith no bigger even than a mustard-seed, you could say to this mulberry-tree, 'Be rooted up and replanted in the sea,' and it would at once obey you" (17:5-6, NEB).

The picture becomes clearer. Jesus was not emphasizing prayer at all, but faith. We go back and reread the Marcan pericope, and suddenly it is evident that "Have faith in God" is the real key to the meaning there. Jesus was not supporting a magical view of prayer. Instead, he was advocating the life of faith that comes from the discipline of prayerful meditation. The power in his own life came from such meditation. It seemed to emanate from his person wherever he went, so that the devils fell down and worshiped him. It did not come from localized, on-the-spot conjuring.

We will experience the same thing in our own lives if we will submit ourselves to the practice of meditative prayer.

Too often we have been frustrated with prayer because we misunderstand how it functions in our lives. We go to pray with a list of items we want to ask of God—what a friend of mine calls "hangnail prayers," prayers about this and that. Then, when nothing happens, when the hangnails persist, we become restless and dissatisfied. "It doesn't work," we think.

Of course it doesn't work that way. God's power, the cosmic power, must flow through us, as it did through Jesus.

And it cannot flow through us until we have been transformed in prayer as Jesus was.

Oh, some minor things may happen. We all possess some power of ESP and PK, and occasionally that will do a small job and astonish us.

But the real power of prayer comes only when we have been changed, when our eyes have been opened and we see the world as God's miracle. The real power comes when we realize that we are surrounded on every side by miracles, and are filled with wonder and awe every moment of the day. Then we are really in touch with the source of power.

In biofeedback terms, we must stop trying to pray so much with the left side of our brains—the objective, activistic side—and learn to pray with the right side, thus developing a personal wholeness we have never known before.

In biblical terms, we must understand that prayer is not a means of educing divine power for specific objectives apart from the concerns of the kingdom of God. The kingdom is the Bible's language for the full realization of God's presence in the world, with all that that entails socially and politically, as well as psychologically. And it is only as the Christian sees the kingdom breaking through around him that he truly experiences the meaning of prayer.

How many times have we prayed for some particular item of desire or urgency, doubting that it would be granted, and then been frustrated that it was not? We begin to disbelieve in the efficacy of prayer. We say the Bible was wrong in what it promised about prayer.

But the Bible was not wrong, for it did not promise what we thought it promised. The Bible does not, except perhaps in some remoter parts, contain an "Open, Sesame" view of prayer.

What it does contain, over and over again, is the picture of how unlimited our power is in the world when we open ourselves to God's giving nature.

Then our prayers for particular objectives become unimportant to us. We are living eucharistically, in perpetual thanksgiving. Gone are our anxieties for the things we once prayed for. Suddenly we see that they are given, they are already ours, at least as sufficiently as we could ask for them.

We take our shoes off and feel the clover on our bare feet.

Life is different.

Prayer becomes praise and thanksgiving. Petition is only secondary, an afterthought.

"*Thy* will be done." Sincerely, joyously.

"*Thy* kingdom."

Thy power.

Thy glory.

How wonderful everything seems to us when our priorities have been reordered this way. How special the world becomes when we relax and enjoy what is already at hand for us, instead of looking to see what our neighbors have, worrying about whether we will have enough for tomorrow, and being concerned about how to get more.

Let me illustrate what I am talking about with the case of a minister friend. This friend had returned to school to work on a graduate degree and was without a pastorate. As he neared the end of his degree program he began to search actively for a new position. He was serving as interim minister at a very modest little church while flying around the country visiting with the pulpit committees of larger and more prestigious churches.

For some reason, the minister was not receiving invitations from these churches to become their pastor, and he was beginning to grow quite anxious about it. Sometimes he knew the persons who *were* invited to become their pastors, and knew that his own qualifications were superior to theirs. What could he do, he wondered, to promote himself into one of these fine positions?

One day in our prayer seminar we discussed the importance of thanksgiving and listening in prayer. This minister decided to go home and try it. Instead of carrying his anxieties about his situation to God, he spent his prayer time recounting the joys in his life and trying to listen to the Spirit.

He came back with startling news! In listening to God, he realized what a delightful little congregation he was already ministering to. They had asked him to be their pastor, but in his ambition for a more notable position he had overlooked them. Now he was suddenly aware of their worth.

To make a long story brief, he accepted a call to the little church and has been exceedingly happy there. He has worked hard and the congregation has responded admirably. His whole life seems to have acquired a new radiance, a new sense of being deeply grounded in faith—all because of what he discovered about thanksgiving and listening.

How many of us could learn a lesson from this, and look with new eyes at our homes, our jobs, our schools, our marriages, our churches, our relationships, our bodies, our faces, our talents, our possessions.

Seeing the miracles and learning to say "Thy will be done" is what prayer is about.

The followers of Jesus in the early church knew this. They prayed abundantly. From the time Jesus left them until the festival of Pentecost, we are told, a group of them numbering 120 were "constantly at prayer." Constantly! It is no wonder that there was an outpouring of Spirit at Pentecost, and that such tremendous crowds responded to the preaching of Simon Peter.

I have said to my preaching students that if they could get only five persons in their churches to pray like that, they would have little Pentecosts every time they come together.

Pentecost became the symbol of what happens when we pray this way. The people experienced a sense of freedom and power they had never known before. They spoke and understood languages they had never spoken or understood before. It was as if tongues of fire danced on their foreheads. They felt so remarkably generous when they saw the miracle of life that they gave all their property to the fellowship to be distributed among the poor and needy among them. What need did they have of it any longer? They had discovered the source of daily bread!

I know that respectable theology looks askance at the description of Pentecost, as if it should not be taken too literally. Surely those were not real flames which touched people's foreheads. And the language thing—there must be some more rational explanation for that.

But what about the right hemisphere of the brain? It is the seat of visual imagery, say the researchers. What if all of those people, through constant prayer and meditation, had brought the right sides of their brains into play? What if they had tapped reservoirs of energy and ability in themselves which lie dormant in all of us until we learn to do the same thing?

Remember the Swami Rama's ability to alter the temperature in his hand.

Perhaps the reality described among the early Christians is greater than the reality we know today because our views of life and nature are so narrowly proscribed by Newtonian physics and Cartesian logic.

The whole question of the resurrection of Jesus, I am convinced, must be addressed along the same line.

Of course the idea of a bodily resurrection, of a man's coming back to life and visiting and dining with friends, is baffling to our modern minds. We are the products of a line of reasoning that admits nothing of life after death because it cannot understand life after death and cannot contain it in mathematical formulas.

But the disciples, bunglers that they were in those final hours, had known something of prayer and meditation during their years with the Master. They may have defected under the tremendous pressure at the last, but what they knew was not lost. It came back to them in a hurry when they saw Jesus again.

Like the child
he sees everything for the first time.
                              —Nikos Kazantzakis
                                Zorba the Greek

Suddenly it was all clear. What he had taught them about the kingdom of God within them was true. They saw the world again as miracle, only more than before. They had not been wrong. It was the others who were wrong—the people who lived by common sense and clamored for special miracles only to have their minds teased or titillated. All of it—the resurrection, Pentecost, the many wonders done wherever the disciples went—was part of the absolute presence of God in his world, a presence which any of us can realize at any time in history.

The disciples obviously learned to pray meditatively as Jesus had, because that is the kind of prayer they continued to use so effectively after his death.

It is unfortunate for Christian history that meditative prayer was a part of their oral tradition but was not enshrined in the Scriptures with the same clarity and precision as the model prayer and other clues to liturgical praying in the early church.

But it is evident from all the allusions to prayer we do have that it was primarily a time of withdrawal in which they opened themselves to God to receive whatever he wished to communicate to them. It was a time of thanksgiving and listening. It was a time of visions. There are numerous references in the Book of Acts, for example, to appearances of Jesus or angels during the disciples' prayers.

Ananias was praying when he was told to go to Saul of Tarsus, and Saul was at prayer when he received the vision of Ananias coming to him (Acts 9:12-17).

Cornelius, the Roman centurion, was praying when he had a vision and was instructed to send men to seek Simon Peter at Joppa. And Peter was at prayer on the rooftop when he received the vision of the animals being let down from heaven in a tarpaulin and was instructed to go to the Gentiles with Cornelius and his friends (Acts 10:1-18).

Paul was at prayer when he had the vision of the man of Macedonia calling him to come to help the people of that country (Acts 16:9); when he had a vision instructing him to remain in Corinth (18:9-10); when he fell into a trance in the Temple and beheld Jesus speaking to him (22:17-18); and probably when he had two later visions, one of Jesus telling him he would live to testify in Rome (23:11), and one of an angel saying that the storm-wracked ship which bore him toward Rome would be brought safely to land (27:23-24).

Are we conscious of a lack of power and divine leadership in the church today? Perhaps it is because we have forgotten how to pray in such a total way. We are so sophisticated. Doesn't it tell us something that the places where the church still appears to be empowered and experiencing miracles today are generally among Pentecostals and lower economic groups which have not been brainwashed by traditional education?

One of my students made an interesting remark after rereading the Book of Acts.

"We're so busy," he said, "that we have to interrupt

what we're doing in order to pray. But God was always having to interrupt the first Christians at their prayer in order to get them to do things!"

It was a telling observation—and the secret of their power. You and I are very activistic. The left sides of our brains predominate in us. We often slight our devotional lives because we assume it is better to be doing something than to be praying. But Jesus and the disciples found power to do what they did because they took time to pray, to listen to God, to feed on the Spirit.

Do you remember the poster with the Eastern flavor a few years ago? It said: "Don't just do something—stand there!"

Maybe that is a message we need to hear.

The power of the early Christians had nothing to do with isolated instances of magic. It was a manifestation of the kingdom of God which they saw opening up like a new world around them. They merely leaned into the winds of the Spirit.

To be sure, there were miraculous events.

When Peter and John reported to the disciples that they had been arraigned before the authorities for an act of healing, the group prayed and the entire building where they were meeting began to shake (Acts 4:31).

On another occasion, when Peter had been imprisoned by Herod, the church prayed for him and an angel appeared to him and led him out of prison (Acts 12:5–12).

And while Paul and Silas were in prison at Philippi, praying and singing praises after midnight, there was a sound like an earthquake and the prison walls collapsed (Acts 16:25).

But all of these events, like those in Jesus' own ministry, seemed to spring more from a new awareness of God's presence than from isolated attempts at producing extraordinary works.

It is noteworthy that not once in the entire Book of Acts is there a single reference to prayer as something an individual does for himself. Always, without fail, it was for the Movement. It was for people to become aware of the kingdom of God in their midst.

How different from our puny attempts to pray!

They were not trying to con God out of anything.

They merely submitted themselves to a rising tide and took the consequences. In many cases it meant hardship, suffering, death. But they recognized *life* when they saw it, and were not afraid to give themselves to it.

Take Paul, for example.

Only once in all his writings is there a reference to his having sought anything through prayer for himself. In 2 Corinthians 12:8-9, he says he asked God three times to remove a certain "sharp pain" in his body.

But this prayer, Paul says, was answered only in the negative: "My grace is all you need; power comes to its full strength in weakness." Grace alone— awareness of all God's wonders.

So Paul stopped at nothing to preach the gospel—not at beatings, not at imprisonment, not at shipwreck, not even at approaching execution. Annoyed at the nagging pain that sometimes hindered him, he cried for God to take it away. But he cried on the run. And, when it wasn't taken away, he exulted all the more in God's grace. Dragging himself on, he marveled that God could use even a partial cripple like himself. What was his pain beside the gift of the kingdom?!

In his great letter to the Romans Paul bewailed his bondage under the law—his plain man's way of looking at life—and asked who could rescue him from "this body doomed to death."

Isn't it a question we are all asking?

God alone can do it, says Paul—through Jesus Christ. Then he exclaims, "Thanks be to God!" (Rom. 7:25, NEB).

"Pray continually," says 1 Thessalonians, a letter either written by Paul or containing fragments of his writings; "give thanks whatever happens; for this is what God in Christ wills for you" (1 Thess. 5:17–18, NEB).

Like Jesus, Paul was a eucharistic man. His eyes beheld the world for what it really was—a basket of miracles.

It is tantalizing to recall how intimately his conversion to Christianity was related to a way of seeing. He had been on the road to Damascus when a flash of light blinded him. He heard the voice of Jesus speaking to him, telling him to go into the city and wait. Led by the others, who had seen and heard nothing, he did as he was told. For three days and nights he fasted and prayed, taking nothing to eat or drink.

When Ananias came to him, he laid his hands on him and said that Jesus had sent him so that Paul might recover his sight and be filled with the Holy Spirit—the two together!

"And immediately," say the Scriptures, "it seemed that scales fell from his eyes, and he regained his sight" (Acts 9:18, NEB).

But there is no doubt he saw differently after that. His whole perspective was changed. Before, he had seen the world as an arena of competition and death, where people wage incessant war against themselves as well as others, trying to get ahead, trying to escape as much suffering as possible, always against incalculable odds. Afterwards, he saw the miracles, a world where God is always cooperating for good with those who love him and are trying to fulfill his purposes in life.

How wonderful life becomes when we see it that way.

Recently, a fine young man from Arizona was in considerable mental agony because his infant daughter was having a serious locomotive problem. It was discovered that one of her hip joints was not growing properly. An operation was planned, and apprehension was mounting in the young man and his wife.

It would be so easy, he wrote in his journal, to see the Lord's Prayer as being greatly out of touch with what really matters to me. It might be more relevant to pray:

> Our Father, who art in heaven,
> why aren't you down here on earth,
> doing something about my present difficulty?
> Who cares if your name is hallowed,
> or whether or not your kingdom comes,
> when what concerns us most
> is what life is really made of—
> our big and little hurts. . . .

But the young man didn't pray that prayer. Instead, he tried to give thanks for his daughter and the joy she had brought into their home. Then, listening for the voice of the Spirit, he reviewed the world around him to see what he could be thankful for. At last, turning again to the Lord's Prayer, he asked himself how he could possibly pray it in relation to the situation that had weighed so heavily on his mind.

This is what he wrote:

Our Father, in spite of the present difficulty,
you are still in heaven and the world is still ordered.
May my response hallow your name.
The coming of your kingdom is more important
    than my own difficulty—so may I not hinder
    its coming by my worry.
Cause this event to be an opening up to
    your will for earth
    which I can see as clearly
    as if I were in heaven.
I must recognize that you still provide
    the necessities of life:
    I have bread enough.
May this event help me to realize how important
    it is to secure your forgiveness
    and to forgive those who have sinned against me.
And may this not be an occasion for temptation
    to lose faith or respond as a pagan.
Deliver me from any evil response or action
    in this difficulty.
The overriding and all-important fact of life
    is that to you belongs the kingdom
    and the power and the glory forever,
    and this event is caught up in that fact.
Amen.

A few days after the young man had come to this new viewpoint the little girl was admitted to the hospital for her operation. I telephoned, thinking I would go to visit the parents during the surgery, but could not locate them. When I saw the young man again, I told him I had tried to reach him.

He was all smiles. Apparently the operation had been deemed successful.

"It was the strangest thing," he said. "They took our daughter for more x-rays the day before surgery was scheduled and her joint had started to grow. They didn't operate. The doctors said it was a miracle! Apparently she's going to be all right."

The immediate person thinks and imagines that when he prays, the important thing, the thing he must concentrate upon, is that God should hear what HE is praying for. And yet in the true, eternal sense it is just the reverse: the true relation in prayer is not when God hears what is prayed for, but when the person praying continues to pray until he is the one who hears, who hears what God wills. The immediate person, therefore, uses many words and, therefore, makes demands in his prayer; the true man of prayer only attends.

—S∮ren Kierkegaard, Journals

3

Prayer

and the Individual

"Sometimes I am afraid to pray," said a friend of mine, "because of what it will do to me."

I understand that. It is a legitimate fear. We are dealing, when we pray, with unlimited forces. And one can get hurt that way.

There is no clearer picture of this than the story of Jesus and the disciples in the Garden of Gethsemane. "Pray that you may be spared the hour of testing," Jesus said to the disciples (Luke 22:40, NEB). They didn't, of course. They slept. But Jesus did pray the prayer. "Father," he said, "if it be thy will, take this cup away from me. Yet not my will but thine be done" (Luke 22:42, NEB).

Jesus' prayer was answered. Not by the removal of the cup, but by the descent of quietude upon his soul. "There appeared to him an angel from heaven bringing him strength," is the way the Bible puts it (Luke 22:43, NEB).

He came from the garden refreshed and decisive, ready for the worst the world could offer.

The disciples, on the other hand, who had slept and might therefore be expected to be refreshed and alert, behaved with alarm and confusion. Peter struck out hastily with his sword, then ran away. The others disappeared too.

I am fond of imagining what might have happened if they had prayed, as Jesus told them to. Would God have said no to them too? Would an angel have ministered to them? Would they too have come forth rested and strengthened, and gone to their own crosses as Jesus did?

I expect so.

They escaped by not praying.

I am reminded of John Magee's analogy in *Reality and Prayer*. He and his family were enjoying a summer holiday along the Pacific northwest coast. There were signs warning them of the danger of bathing except when the tide was coming in, and they obeyed the signs. But many times, as Magee watched his wife and children disappear beneath the foam of a breaker, he felt his heart catch in fear. He thought of the tremendous depths from which the ocean's power flowed, and of the weakness of the most powerful swimmer against those churning forces. His loved ones, he knew, could be carried away in a moment.

It is the same with prayer. The power is inestimable. We can be swept away in an instant, never to stand again precisely where we stood before.

The secret is in what the New Testament calls *metanoia* or conversion. *Metanoia*—going beyond our present mind. Something happens. A hidden spring is touched. We stop going against the current and simply flow with it. We become aligned with the will of God for the world.

Jesus was very adept at this. He meditated until he was perfectly aligned. "I and the Father are one," he said.

In terms of the western philosophical experience, it has to do with getting our objective and subjective natures back together again, so that life is unified.

We have tended, for too many years, to practice a debilitating kind of dualism between our minds and our bodies, our thoughts and our feelings, what is outside us and what is inside us. We erect partitions which divide us against ourselves and against the world we live in. Movement becomes difficult. The flow of power is interrupted.

But prayer brings the walls down, uniting our beings again. We can feel life becoming whole once more. We know we are connected to the power again. It flows through us as though we were its natural conduits. We feel clean, open, generous, ready to give all that we have—even our lives—to the power.

This is what Jesus did in Gethsemane. He prayed away his own inner obstructions to the force of God. It is why he came out so refreshed and ready to meet the challenge of the priests and Pharisees. He felt his unity with the Father.

Openness to the power was a constant theme in Jesus' teachings. It informed everything he said about wealth and greed for possessions. The earth is free, he advised, and we should live freely in it. It is when we begin to draw boundaries and build walls that we begin to destroy ourselves and die. Nothing should block the flow of God's life-bestowing force in the world.

Consider this passage from the Sermon on the Mount:

> Do not store up for yourselves treasure on earth, where it grows rusty and moth-eaten, and thieves break in to steal it. Store up treasure in heaven, where there is no moth and no rust to spoil it, no thieves to break in and steal. For where your treasure is, there will your heart be also.
>
> The lamp of the body is the eye. If your eyes are sound, you will have light for your whole body; if the eyes are bad, your whole body will be in darkness. If then the only light you have is darkness, the darkness is doubly dark.
>
> No servant can be slave to two masters; for either he will hate the first and love the second, or he will be devoted to the first and think nothing of the second. You cannot serve God and Money (Matt. 6:19–24, NEB).

At first the part about the eye seems out of place. Why should it stand thus between two paragraphs about possessions? Because, it has been explained, people in Jesus' day connected the *eye* with money the way we connect the *hand* with it. Instead of a person's being "tight-fisted" or "open-handed" with possessions, he had an eye that was "bad" or "sound."

Jesus was saying, in other words, that we cannot be grudging, niggardly stewards of the earth and really enjoy the power of God. The power must flow through us without impediment. It must flow freely, easily, gracefully. If we try to grasp at life, we lose it. But if we renounce ownership of it and simply accept it as it comes, always giving thanks for it, then we are never without it.

Living this way is identical with what early Christians called "living in the Spirit." By spending much time in prayer, they learned to let life flow without trying to grasp it. They did not worry themselves with future plans. They were assured that the Spirit would tell them what to say if they were brought before magistrates and rulers. They simply waited on the power of God, thereby tapping resources they might otherwise have missed.

Transcendental meditation attempts to lead its disciples into the same kind of fullness by advising them to get connected with the deepest source of Being before any kind of act.

"It is not necessary to plan how to behave," says Maharishi Mahesh, "it is not necessary to think much about how to behave, what to do, how to speak, or how to handle a situation. Let the situation come, handle it innocently and naturally. If the practice of transcendental deep meditation is regular and sustained, all behavior on all levels will naturally be rewarding."

Life, says Maharishi Mahesh, is like shooting an arrow. Before the arrow can rush forward, it must be drawn back on the string. If it is not drawn back, it will fall limply from the archer's hand. Similarly, we are able to live at our full potential only as we withdraw regularly to the source of power.

There is no difference between this and Jesus' life or what he commended to the disciples. The power comes from living with God. Only as we pray do we become the free and open conductors of grace in the world.

Through prayer, our deepest natures are converted to God. We learn to hinder him less and less, until it seems almost that his very nature is within us and his slightest wish is our command.

In a sense, we even become the God we pray to. By meditating on him, our beings merge with his until there is no boundary between them. We are one with him, as Christ is. His power, his grace, his love flow unstintedly through us. It is the greatest single mystery of our faith.

Gradually our entire character and demeanor are shaped by God. Like the young man in Hawthorne's story of "The Great Stone Face," who admired the sculpture on the cliff until he resembled it, we become the mirrors of God. People behold his glory in our faces. They see him in the freedom and generosity with which we live.

The author of the famous conversations with Brother Lawrence witnesses to this remarkable transparency in that simple monk's life:

> As Brother Lawrence had found such an advantage in walking in the presence of God, it was natural for him to recommend it earnestly to others; but his example was a stronger inducement than any arguments he could propose. His very countenance was edifying, such a sweet and calm devotion appearing in it as could not but affect the beholders. And it was observed that in the greatest hurry of business in the kitchen he still preserved his recollection and heavenly-mindedness. He was never hasty nor loitering, but did each thing in its season, with an even, uninterrupted composure and tranquillity of spirit. "The time of business," said he, "does not with me differ from the time of prayer; and in the noise and clatter of my kitchen, while several persons are at the same time calling for different things, I possess God in as great tranquillity as if I were upon my knees at the blessed sacrament."

Such tranquillity and openness to the power of God, of course, do not usually come to us instantly. Even

Brother Lawrence's letters, and the conversations which are set down with them, are entitled *The Practice of the Presence of God.*

Conversion is a process. It works deeper and deeper, like an acid, until it has altered our most secret depths. Not even a lifetime is long enough for it to complete its work. This is why we should not dismiss too lightly the idea of purgatory, a state beyond mortality in which the soul is further prepared for the presence of God, or the notion of some psychics that the dead often linger near the place of death while being tutored for their acceptance into the afterlife.

The discipline of prayer by which conversion is effected may vary considerably, of course, depending on personal temperament.

There is the discipline of the person under holy orders who prays for hours every day, turning the bread of this world into something more substantial, something holy, visited by Christ. It is not fake, as a doctor friend of mine seems to think. *Orare est laborare,* as the ancient phrase has it: to pray is to work. There is no work that is harder or more valuable.

But there is also the discipline of a man like Frank Laubach, the famous apostle of literacy, who prayed as he read the newspaper, as he ate his meals, as he watched people in a railway station.

"Hmmm," he would say, reading about some ambassador or prime minister in difficulty, "God strengthen him for his tasks today."

"What burdens is that woman in front of me bearing?" he pondered as he rode from one city to another, from one speaking engagement to another. "God, brighten her day."

And I believe him when he says the woman turned around to speak to him, merely from having a prayer beamed at the back of her head. I believe him—where I might not believe another—because of the magnificent work the man did to bring his literacy program to hundreds of thousands of people in the darkest nations on earth. He was too busy to go to a monastery to pray, so he prayed as he went, and it kept converting his life as effectively as if he had been a monk.

People said his face shone with the light of the gospel. Everything he wrote shone with it too.

Prayer is not talking to God
but listening to God talking to you.

—Louis Evely
Our Prayer

Even the smallest efforts at discipline are not without reward. One Holy Week when I had to be away, I requested that my students spend their class time praying, and report on their experience the next time we met. One likable young man who said he couldn't pray had gone to Centennial Park and whiled away two hours watching the ducks.

"I don't dig prayer very much," he said, "but that time in the park had a distinct effect in my life. I felt this huge sense of serenity come over me, and things seemed to go into place for me, all my assignments and everything. It was great!"

The effect of such an occasional time of serenity soon wears away, of course. The real secrets of prayer become known through long discipline earnestly worked at.

Bernanos understood this in *The Diary of a Country*

Priest. "The usual notion of prayer is so absurd," he wrote.

> How can those who know nothing about it, who pray little or not at all, dare speak so frivolously of prayer? A Carthusian, a Trappist will work for years to make of himself a man of prayer, and then any fool who comes along sets himself up as judge of this lifelong effort. If it were really what they suppose, a kind of chatter, the dialogue of a madman with his shadow, or even less—a vain and superstitious sort of petition to be given the good things of this world—how could innumerable people find until their dying day sheer, robust, vigorous, abundant joy in prayer? Oh, of course, "suggestion," say the scientists. Certainly they can never have known old monks, wise, shrewd, unerring in judgment, and yet aglow with passionate insight, so very tender in their humanity. What miracle enables these semi-lunatics, these prisoners of their own dreams, these sleep-walkers, apparently to enter more deeply each day into the pain of others?

"Could a sane man," asks Bernanos, "set himself up as a judge of music because he has sometimes touched a keyboard with the tips of his fingers?"

We marvel at Jesus' prayer in Gethsemane. How could anyone facing the dread probability of imminent death so fortify himself with an hour's worth of prayer as to emerge refreshed and resourceful? The answer is, of course, that Jesus did not only pray occasionally, when he felt the need of it. He was a man of prayer. His whole being, his very fiber, had been daily strengthened by prayer for years.

There was no thrashing about in Gethsemane for a one-time contact with the source of all power. Jesus slipped naturally into the role of prayer, the way a practiced athlete slips quickly into his playing style.

How much time is required of us each day if we are to know the way prayer really works?

Transcendental meditation and yoga both ask at least fifteen minutes twice a day. If you will fix your mind on a proper mantra, or phrase for meditation, they say, you will become a new person within weeks.

This seems minimal. However, personalities vary, and the time required for prayer as well as the mode in which the praying is done will differ from person to person.

The important thing is the intensity. In Jesus' day, this was called *kawwanah,* or the quality of concentration. What must happen is that the prayer, brief or long as it is, must set the tone for everything else in your life.

One of my students a few years ago was the wife of a dairy farmer. She and her husband rose at 4:30 each morning to milk their cows. During our prayer seminar, she decided that she needed more time each day for a deliberate meditative act. So she began rising at 4:00 and spending 30 minutes in prayer before going to the barn.

"Just made a startling discovery!" she wrote one day in her journal. "The time on my knees each morning is the *preparation* for prayer—the rest of the day then *becomes* the prayer!"

That is when prayer really becomes effective—when it converts life itself into praying.

The great Christian doctor Paul Tournier had a similar experience with prayer. For some time he had wished to establish a pattern of meditation in his life, but, as a busy physician, had simply not found the time. Then one day he heard a Dutchman, an official of the League of Nations, refer to the importance of daily devotions in his hurried routine. Surely, thought Tournier, if an important statesman could find the time for prayer each day, then he could do as well.

The next morning, rising with the alarm an hour before usual, Tournier went into his study and sat at his desk. He lay his pocket watch out and commenced to pray, thinking he would engage himself thus for an hour.

When it seemed that the hour must be up, only a few minutes had elapsed! The next time he looked at the watch, it was the same. It was, he said, the most agonizing hour he had ever spent. He thought it would never end.

Finally, when the hour was over, he started to rise, disappointed in himself that nothing had happened. But he obeyed a fleeting impulse to remain at the desk a few moments longer.

And it was in those moments, said Tournier, the ones after the hour was up, that God visited his heart. God had used the hour, he was convinced, as a mere test of obedience. The rewards came in the brief time which followed.

The flavor of that brief time changed Tournier's entire day. It seemed to distill itself into everything he did, even the matters of routine business.

From that day forward, a time of meditation became a regular part of his schedule. Nothing else, he said, had ever enriched his life so much.

When your life becomes centered on God through prayer you feel a new attitude toward everything. The power at the heart of the universe seems to flow through you, sweeping you along toward its own destination. You no longer have to worry about maneuvering this way and that, trying to make things work.

As the Apostle Paul said, everything seems to work together in your favor.

It doesn't mean that you will suddenly be discovered, like Cinderella, and become the belle of the ball, or that your business will prosper and you will become a millionaire. The gospel was never about that.

What it does mean is that you will begin to discover the enormous riches and resources already at your fingertips. You will realize how blind you have been to the amazing treasures that now surround you. You will begin to see as you have never seen before. You will see life in technicolor, not just black and white, and will pinch yourself to see if you aren't dreaming.

There is an ancient Chinese saying, "Before one studies Ch'an (Zen), he sees mountains as mountains and rivers as rivers. When he has received instruction from a master, he no longer sees mountains as mountains and rivers as rivers. But when he has finally come to his own enlightenment, he once more sees mountains as mountains and rivers as rivers."

Most of us enter that middle period when we leave childhood. We no longer see things for what they really are. A mountain becomes a deposit of ore, and a river becomes an avenue of commerce. The magic vanishes, and we are left with problems, challenges, burdens. The paradise disappears, and we wake up in a wilderness.

Prayer brings the paradise back. We marvel at mountains and rivers again—and flowers and trees and birds and horses and stones and rain and stars and everything else. We become filled once more with the elemental wonder that things *are,* not at what they are, which is more the question of the analytical mind.

Many people apparently have the wrong idea about prayer, that it makes one terribly serious and sad about life, and thus distant from the pleasures and joys of existence.

Nothing could be further from the truth! As proof, here is a statement written by an anonymous friar at a monastery in Nebraska—someone whose very being has become converted through prayer:

> If I had my life to live over, I'd try to make more mistakes next time. I would relax, I would limber up, I would be sillier than I have been this trip. I know of a very few things I would take seriously. I would be less hygienic. I would take more chances. I would take more trips. I would climb more mountains, swim more rivers and watch more sunsets. I would eat more ice cream. I would have actual troubles and fewer imaginary ones.
>
> You see, I am one of those people who lives prophylactically and sensibly and sanely, hour after hour, day after day. Oh, I have had my moments and, if I had it to do over again, I'd have more of them. In fact, I'd try to have nothing else. Just moments, one after another, instead of living so many years ahead each day. I have been one of those people who never go anywhere without a thermometer, a hot water bottle, a gargle, a raincoat and a parachute. If I had it to do over again, I would go places and do things and travel lighter than I have.
>
> If I had my life to live over again, I would start barefooted earlier in the spring and stay that way later in the fall. I would play hooky more. I wouldn't make such good grades except by accident. I would ride on more merry-go-rounds. I would pick more daisies.

You say, But I thought Christianity was about saving people's souls, and all of that.

The friar's words *are* about salvation, aren't they? They possess the same kind of absurd vision, the same childlike unreality, as the biblical metaphors of the lion lying down with the lamb and the ox feeding with the bear. Only here the redemption has already occurred, and the writer is saying what he would have done if it had happened years before. He would have spent more time picking daisies.

This is what happens in the discipline of prayer. You begin to acquire a new sensitivity to your world. It becomes bright and effervescent. Things you had not noticed come to your attention. Mountains, rivers, sunsets. Then ice cream, the feel of the grass on your bare feet, and the daisies.

You give up the world to enter into God and let him enter into you, and you really find the world. You surrender the wilderness and discover paradise.

I cannot forget a book of photographs I saw once in a bookstore. They were made with Thomas Merton's camera. The pictures trembled with sensitivity. Deeply etched bark on old trees seemed to live, even on the paper. The dents and scratches in a heavy milk pail imparted a strange density of character to it. Ribbons of ice along the edges of a winter creek shone in the sunlight like the jeweled hem of a royal petticoat spread across the landscape.

The years of bowing in prayer were responsible. Silence and mystery had given birth to a new way of seeing and feeling the world. There was no escapism in Merton, no gnostic otherworldliness. He could not have been more in the world than he was. Holiness had made the world his.

It is the same with people as with things. Prayer makes them more important. Their faces and stories assume a new reality.

"There would be no idiots and no bores for us," wrote the aged Mauriac, "if we could see far enough into this part of them, the part which You know and where You are, if it is a soul in a state of grace where You reside."

Seeing "far enough" is generally the problem. We are so prone to judge persons quickly and superficially, without meditating on them until we know their inner beings. We seldom wait to discern the hidden springs that activate them and provide the surface motions.

"Pray for your enemies," Jesus said.

He said it because it is impossible. The minute you pray for an enemy, he is no longer an enemy, but a brother. The prayer is thrown over him like a cloak of relationship. The situation is altered, transmuted.

The enemy may not realize it immediately, but something has changed. We are not, for him at least, who we were. We have begun to see with new eyes. Soon other things must change too—things outside us, things between us, things in the world.

One of my student friends, who is a minister from Oklahoma, wrote this in his journal:

> Lord, was that You I gave the dollar to last night? In the semi-darkness, was that You or Rodriguez, half-drunk with the suffering of this world?
>
> Was that You asking for a quarter or a half-dollar to buy a taco? Was that You, so bruised and pitiable, who kept trying to convince me that your name was Carlos Rodriguez from Texas?
>
> Haven't I met You like that before? If I have, it

disturbs me that You go around in shadows dirty and half-drunk.

You know, don't You, that it is hard to recognize You in that condition? I guess I want You out of the shadows so I can see You more clearly. Do You really have to go so incognito in our world?

What's that, Lord? What are You saying about being hungry and thirsty? Oh!

When we pray for the kingdom to come, we are asking to be able to see God at work in all kinds of people—derelicts and pariahs, revolutionaries and enemies—and to be able to sit down at table with all of these.

After all, it is his kingdom, not ours. He decides who will be invited. We learn to see the other guests through his eyes. Otherwise we are like the elder son in the parable, unable to receive as brother one who has been welcomed home by the Father.

The kingdom comes inch by inch and foot by foot. The lion and the lamb, the ox and the bear, you and your brother or sister. It happens when you pray. You become more and more adept at seeing it.

A word of practical advice: When you pray, try to talk less and listen more. Wait until the silence forms its soft mantle about you. "Hold yourself in prayer before God," said Brother Lawrence, "like a dumb or paralytic beggar at a rich man's gate." Let the rich man come to you, and his very coming will be heaven.

Consciously will that the right hemisphere of the brain, with its power to visualize, relax, and make contact with the source of Being, predominate over the left hemisphere and its penchant for verbalization and action.

*Experiencing the present
purely is being emptied and hollow;
you catch grace as a man
fills his cup under a waterfall.*

—Annie Dillard
Pilgrim at Tinker Creek

Come boldly into the presence of God, as the writer to the Hebrews expressed it.

Only do not try to bring all your baggage with you.

We are too prone, in the Western world, to bring all our problems to God. We regard prayer as a time for untangling the messes we have made. We think of it as a ouija board for reaching difficult decisions.

Try leaving everything behind.

Be like the Basque sheepherder who always prayed, "Lord, here is John."

Afterwards, or near the end of prayer, the disordered ends of your existence will fall more easily into place. Decisions will be easier to make.

But during the prayer itself, simply steep your soul in God. Let him roll over you like the waves of the ocean. Drift with him this way and that. Become one with him.

Because the right hemisphere of the brain is inclined to images, you may wish to try to relax through certain figures of the mind.

You may wish to imagine yourself, for example, as a piece of driftwood in the ocean.

Or a baby bird being fed by its mother.

Or a field of grain being played over by the wind.

You may also wish sometime to concentrate upon a mantra or saying, as many persons in yoga or Zen do. Maharishi Mahesh advises his followers in transcendental meditation to select a mantra especially suited to their individual natures.

The famous "Jesus prayer"—merely repeating the name Jesus over and over and over—has been used by many mystics through the years. Some say it has great power to chase away the devils from the mind and spirit, so that the person praying experiences deep inner freedom and relaxation.

Christians have long used biblical verses or sayings in the same manner. As Merton has said in his book *Contemplative Prayer* regarding the manner of praying among medieval monastics:

> Prayer was drawn from the Scriptures, especially from the Psalms. The first monks looked upon the Psalter not only as a kind of compendium of all the other books of the Bible, but as a book of special efficacy for the ascetic life, in that it revealed the secret movements of the heart in its struggle against the forces of darkness. The "battle Psalms" were all interpreted as referring to the inner war with passion and with the demons. Meditation was above all *meditatio scripturarum.* But we must not imagine the early monks applying themselves to a very intellectual and analytical "meditation" of the Bible. Meditation for them consisted in making the words of the Bible their own by memorizing them and repeating them, with deep and simple concentration, "from the heart."

Jesus himself, I am sure, meditated often in a similar manner on phrases and sentences from the Old Testament. It was out of such brooding upon the texts that he then spoke to "sharpen" their meaning among his followers.

I have known several persons to benefit, in prayer, from concentrating on objects of the natural world, such as a piece of fruit, a flower, or a stone.

I talked once with a man in Las Vegas who confessed a great partiality to stones. Sometimes, he said, he would drive up into the desert and collect several stones. Then, sitting quietly on a rock, he would wait until he got a special feeling for one. Holding that stone in his hand, he would let his mind drift back through the ages, trying to feel himself present aeons and aeons ago at the time of the stone's formation. It had a great stilling effect on his life, he said, during the periods when his business was most hectic. Often he would bring the stone home with him and repeat the meditation with it for several weeks before returning to the desert again.

My own predilection is for water. When I was a boy, I could sit for hours staring at the surface of a small pond on my father's property, or watching the stones and leaves and crayfish tracks beneath the clear water of a little stream. After I became a Christian, my praying often centered on these objects. There was no pantheism involved. I simply felt surrounded by the glory of God in his creation.

Today, I never get near a body of water without feeling the stir of similar emotions. There is something about the basic elements—earth, air, fire, water—that draws me instinctively to God.

People too are wonderful objects of meditative prayer. Try holding them in your thoughts sometimes as you pray. Let your mind play across them like a camera, taking in their varied moods and outward appearances. Then focus for a few minutes on one person at a time. Feel what psychics call the "aura" of the person—the field of magnetism created by a living soul. Let what is inside the person communicate with you. Listen for the glory of God in one of his children.

Try this especially with people you have no particular liking for, or people who have failed to impress you in any way. You may be surprised at the consequences.

I sat in a hospital room recently and watched an old woman eating.

She was grossly overweight. Great gobs of flesh hung flaccidly about her throat and torso. Her arms were like pale hams.

She had been there seven weeks already.

"Pneumonia," she said.

She had had it not once, but twice. Her old legs were still cut and bruised where she had been fed by tubes.

She was almost lifeless now. Big hulk of a woman, collapsed over her folded arms at a desk where they had set her up. Head down, ragged grey hair akimbo, saying nothing. Then back to bed, wheezing and groaning.

I watched her eat. No talking. Cheeks bulging rhythmically, lips doubling back on one another as toothless gums met to grind the food. A face intent on its job. Only the eyes staring out, seeing, comprehending.

Eat and defecate, said Beckett. Dish and pot. The two extremities of human existence.

I loved the old woman, whom I had only met. I loved the simple face, the working jaws, the heap of body.

I saw in her, watching her eat, the image of God.

You begin to see that way after a while. It is what

prayer does to you. You see God everywhere, in places you never suspected him of being. In burned-down candles, in dogs licking their repulsive sores, in dirty dishes after the meal, in unmade beds, in old people vegetating in hospital wards.

He has been there all the time, of course. You just get to seeing differently.

Maybe you aren't more sensitive to things and people at all. Maybe what you are is more sensitive to God. Maybe you just find out that you haven't been away from him at all, that you can't get away from him, or couldn't if you wanted to, because he is in everything everywhere, only waiting to be seen, waiting to be heard, waiting to be known and loved.

We talk about how difficult love is. Perhaps that is because we don't pray. When you pray, you can't help loving. In fact, praying *is* loving. It is loving the world and loving God through the world. It is even loving the self, for in prayer the self is seen as God sees it, tenderly, redemptively, joyously.

You will possibly go through a period of difficulty in prayer before all of this happens. Monastics know it by the name assigned to it by St. John of the Cross: "the dark night of the soul." It is a strange season of depression which usually settles upon the one praying after he or she has undergone a rather long discipline of meditation—sometimes after years. The dark night will end, but at the time it is very distressing.

Those who know say that this period is most characterized by dread, or what the existentialists call *Angst.* You experience an overwhelming sense of personal unworthiness, almost to the point of dysfunction. You lose the conviction that even God can care for you or reengender enthusiasm in you.

"It is as if God himself were hostile and implacable," says Merton, "or, worse still, as if God himself had become emptiness, and as if all were emptiness, nothingness, dread and night."

The apparent reason for this agony is that the soul goes through a period when it is relinquishing its former images of God, which are mainly anthropomorphic, and coming to apprehend God as imageless, wearing none of the protean masks we have given him. It is a terrifying time, for the changeover is immensely important and far-reaching in its implications. Suddenly God is not what you had imagined at all, and the realization is devastating. He is more than you had imagined, of course; but for the moment that is no comfort to your soul flailing in darkness.

What you discover about God during this dark night is what Meister Eckhardt called his *Istigkeit*—his *is-ness*. Tillich, who studied the mystics, called it the Ground of Being.

The discomfort arises because, in our humanness, we try to apprehend God in metaphorical terms, as Father, as Shepherd's Staff, as Everlasting Arms. Then, in despair at our own unworthiness, we know that such terms are wholly inadequate. God is not human. He transcends such language or visualization. He simply is, and his *is-ness* is nearly unbearable.

If you persist through this black period, however, waiting tenaciously even when there is no sufficient mental representation of the Being who inhabits the darkness, your reward is the memory of the *is-ness* for the rest of your life. For there is something irrevocable about this intense experience. Its essence lingers in the mind and heart, and, like the odor of some exotic flower, perfumes even the darkest corridors of your future existence.

You will never again be utterly troubled by aloneness or unbelief. However dark the night you tread, you will feel with a certain tangibility the brooding presence of the One you encountered as darkness. Imagelessness will no longer make you doubt. You will take comfort from it, as if meeting a friend. You will relish the silence, and find it more pregnant than speech. It will be like the intimacy experienced by old married persons, for whom a glance says volumes and understanding passes like an air wave, mute as the space between them.

Strangely enough, you will feel more comfortable with your humanness than ever before. Having found God to be more than human, you will see that humanity is part of your creatureliness, and that God not only accepts it but blesses it. You will be able to call God "Father" when you pray without worrying about whether it is an adequate designation or whether, as Freud suggested, you are indulging in a "wish-projection" for a superhuman parent. You will smile inwardly at your own weakness, knowing that it merely leaves more strength to God.

You will no longer despair of loving God or being loved by him. Your very helplessness will increase your sense of childlike dependence on him and your feelings of affection for him and the world he sustains.

Years ago I copied out of one of Menninger's books some words reprinted from the diary of Father William Doyle, a Jesuit chaplain who was killed at the battlefront in 1917. I have reread them many times. "I long to get back to my little room at night," he wrote, "to calm and quiet, and yet I dread it, for He is often so loving there. . . . It is such a helpless feeling to be tossed about, as it were, on the waves of love, to feel the ardent, burning love of His heart, to know He asks for love, and then to realize one human heart is so tiny. . . . At times I feel half mad with the love of God. . . . Every fiber of His divine nature is thrilling with love for me . . . every beat of His gentle heart is a throb of intense affection for me."

What serenity must have accompanied that man on the battlefield. He was like a child whose father held his hand through every danger.

Was he naïve, immature, romantic?

Or had he passed through his dark night of the soul to the luminous years beyond?

The latter, I think.

He was what you will grow into when you pray—a person so convinced of the love of God in your life that you will walk without fear or distraction in the valley of deepest shadows. He was so transformed by meditation that no storm could confuse the needle of his soul. It always knew where True North was. What to others was a bloody nightmare of a wilderness was to him a paradise.

"We are no better than pots of earthenware to contain this treasure," said St. Paul, "and this proves that such transcendent power does not come from us, but is God's alone. Hard-pressed on every side, we are never hemmed in; bewildered, we are never at our wits' end; hunted, we are never abandoned to our fate; struck down, we are not left to die. Wherever we go we carry death with us in our body, the death that Jesus died, that in this body also life may reveal itself, the life that Jesus lives. . . . No wonder we do not lose heart! Though our outward humanity

is in decay, yet day by day we are inwardly renewed"
(2 Cor. 4:7-10,16, NEB).

Alone, you are a fragile vessel. But, filled with the
Spirit of God, there is nothing in the world that can
beat you.

I remember prostrating myself at night, and feeling the cool of the wooden floor against my forehead. Soul and body became one in those times, united like Dürer's famous praying hands. The effect was somewhat similar to what Zen Buddhists claim for the lotus position in their meditations. They say the spine then is something like a tree planted in the earth, and the body teaches the mind what it may have forgotten, to relax with nature, to commune with the universe. Only bowing for prayer reflects a theological commitment that is missing from meditation of any other kind: the body becomes an arrow pointing to the deity, a tongue praising his name. This is very important.

In Zen, the disciple is trying to get in touch with something basic that is already here, that is present in the universe as it is; that is the whole aim of his devotion. In Christianity, the disciple is also seeking connection with something already here. But in his case what is already here is also coming. It is the kingdom that has come and is coming. It is what God has given to every individual who will accept it, but what he has yet for the world when the world will receive it.

The eschatological dream of every Zen Buddhist is one man alone in a meadow enjoying tranquillity. The dream of the Christian is of all men together with God in their midst. And, as I was going to say, the bowing in prayer reflects this.

—From an earlier draft of Bread for the
Wilderness, Wine for the Journey

4

Prayer

and the Community

Almost every book about prayer written in the last hundred years has been addressed to the individual, as if prayer were an essentially private part of religion. Yet the records of the early church seem to indicate that corporate prayer—praying together—occupied fully as much time as individual prayer.

The Lord's Prayer, which served as a catechetical device to teach new converts how to pray, is pointedly communal: *"Our* Father . . . give *us* this day *our* daily bread . . . forgive *us* . . . as *we* forgive . . . lead *us* not into temptation but deliver *us* from evil."

And we know that the disciples continued for many years to join in prayer at the Jewish canonical hours for praying, morning, noon, and evening.

It is hard to imagine what Christianity might have become—or failed to become—if it had not been for this liturgical discipline which the earliest Christians continued to share.

Jesus himself provided the example of a kind of rhythm between prayer alone and prayer with the group. He often withdrew to pray in secret, and we suppose that these were times when he prayed listening, letting the Spirit play over him like some master player tuning an instrument.

But Jesus obviously prayed too with the disciples. Despite their faulty performance the night of the Last Supper, we are told it was *their* custom, not Jesus' alone, to repair to Gethsemane for prayer.

What the disciples learned from him is evident in the Book of Acts; alone or in groups, they were constantly at prayer.

After more than three thousand people were added to the church at Pentecost, they met daily "to hear the apostles teach, and to share the common life, to break bread, and to pray" (Acts 2:42, NEB). They prayed together whenever they laid hands on deacons to ordain them or appointed elders in each locality. They prayed for the sick and imprisoned. They prayed for the new churches, and for the missionaries who were working to establish the gospel. And, mostly, they simply prayed in praise and adoration.

Prayer, for the first Christians, was an experience of joy and ecstasy. It was where they felt the unique Spirit of God and became acquainted with resources of power in themselves and their world which they had not known before. It was a time of dreams and visions, all associated with the discovery of the kingdom in their midst.

It is little wonder that such prayer was for them a communal event even more than it was a private one. The psychology of the Hebrew people had always inclined toward the corporate. They regarded the *nephesh* or soul of a person as the center of a network extending far beyond the boundaries of the individual, including his or her family, chattel, land, and everything else related to the person's identity. In the Old Testament, this way of thinking stemmed from the corporate fate of the Israelites; they were the people of God, and he dealt with them at a corporate or national level. In the New Testament, the nation was transcended by the kingdom of God, and individualism was still submerged in the corporate entity. Even if there had not been the pressures of defamation and persecution, which naturally produce solidarity, the early Christians would have prayed in groups; it was in their nature to do so.

Ours, by contrast, is a time of anti-community. Something has happened to life in our age. It seems fragmented, multiple, divided. Our literature is full of *isolatoes*, poor Kafkaesque figures who have lost touch with other human beings. We are more transient and rootless than the ancient nomads. When they moved, they took their families with them—all the aunts and uncles and cousins. But the extended family is fast becoming a thing of the past for us. Technology and urbanization have all but destroyed old concepts of neighborliness and friendship. Even churches and synagogues suffer from the disappearance of the old parish concept, for their clienteles usually come from miles around and the people see little of each other from one weekend to the next. Everywhere today the talk is of alienation, loneliness, lack of community.

Everywhere, that is, except where people pray together.

Nothing creates community the way prayer does. Prayer's vision is of the kingdom, unity, and love. It is of the lion lying down with the lamb, and the infant child playing harmlessly at the hole of the adder. It is of the nations bowing around the throne of God, dancing and singing praises until there are no more strangers and there is no more loneliness.

Our rhythm of prayer, like that of Jesus and the disciples, ought to reflect this by being both private and communal. There should be time for quiet reflection, for meditation, for listening to God; and there should be time for group prayers, for communal praise and worship. The two belong together and necessarily complement one another. Private prayer without corporate prayer tends to degenerate into subjectivism, romanticism, and magicalism; corporate prayer without private prayer usually becomes cold, mechanical, and merely repetitive.

Thomas Merton, who was a great student of prayer, understood the reciprocity between spontaneous private devotion and the set prayers of public ritual. "Liturgy by its very nature tends to prolong itself in individual contemplative prayer," he said, "and mental prayer in its turn disposes us for and seeks fulfillment in liturgical worship."

The two are mutually dependent. One stokes the fires of the other. We neglect either at the peril of the other. The early Christians found it so natural to move from one to the other and back again that they did not even think to offer succeeding generations any rules for relating or balancing them. The one thing important to them was always to pray "in the Spirit." That way they were invariably sure of the passion and significance of prayer regardless of the method employed.

Forsyth summed it up soundly in his little book *The Soul of Prayer*. There is no better preparation for public prayer, he said, than private prayer. The vulgarity of so many prayers said in churches proceeds more from a lack of the *habit* of prayer than from inferior rhetorical ability. One can tell it in the very atmosphere of a prayer, in the very air it breathes. Even a prayer composed by a gifted theologian or a communications expert will be hollow and tedious if it has not been preceded by the discipline of prayer in the composer's own life.

On the other hand, argued Forsyth, "We are saved in a common salvation. The atmosphere of prayer is communion. Common prayer is the inevitable fruit of a gospel like Christ's." Therefore even our private prayer should be common in spirit. "It is common prayer, however solitary, that prevails as being most in tune with the great first goal of God's grace—the community."

Here is the nub of the matter. The goal of God's grace is the community—the kingdom. Christian prayer, whether individual or common, should be directed toward this end. If it is, its spirit will be the same whether it is private or public. The one who prays will not feel a disruption when moving from one to the other. Instead, as Merton said, he or she will find each extending itself in the other. Common prayer will require the additional payment of time in private, and private prayer will find its true fulfillment in the prayer of the group.

There is an illustration of this reflexive relationship in the journal of the friend to whom I have already alluded, who helps her husband to manage a dairy farm. She became a Christian several years ago through the church's ministry of public worship. Yet, convinced that she needed a more disciplined life of meditation herself, she began rising half an hour earlier in order to pray. She wrote, at that time:

> If I, who am nothing,
>   cannot take time
>   out of each day
>   for God—
> why then should I expect God
>   in all his great glory
>   to take time out
>   for me?

At first she found it very difficult to rise so early— she and her husband were already arising long before daylight. "It is so *hard* to keep my appointment with God every morning," she wrote.

But it became easier.

She prayed mostly for others—for friends, for family, for the President, for the church, for classroom acquaintances.

And she listened.

Then, less than a month from the day she began the prayer time, she entered these words in her diary:

"Our worship service was one of ecstasy! The sound of my husband's singing (he seldom joins in singing) brought real tears of joy and thanksgiving! And the whole atmosphere was one of prayer. So different from so many services. Must remember to ask the minister if he felt it. Somehow think he did from remark he made from pulpit. What a joyous occasion, this communion Sunday! Did not want it to end. One of the most moving experiences in recent years. A renewal, a promise.

"Wonder if my return to a daily communion with

God has anything to do with it? I expect so!"

Subsequent entries in the journal indicate that the worship service in turn became part of the gathering momentum of the author's prayer life and experience with God. Prayer became praise, and praise became prayer. It is the reciprocal relationship of which both Merton and Forsyth have spoken.

Imagine an entire congregation of people having the same experience. That is precisely what resulted in the original experience of Christian Pentecost. The disciples, after Jesus parted from them near Bethany, returned to Jerusalem in a joyful spirit "and spent all their time in the temple praising God" (Luke 24:53, NEB). Together with a group of women and Jesus' mother and brothers, they prayed constantly for weeks, until the time of the Jewish festival of Pentecost.

Is it any wonder, after this, that the Spirit of God fell upon them, so that they felt and did unusual things, or that Simon Peter the fisherman was able to stand and deliver one of the greatest sermons ever preached?

Frank Laubach once said that Christianity is doomed unless it somehow rediscovers that "the center and power of its divine service is prayer, not sermons; God, not the preacher." It makes a great difference, he noted, if the preacher even asks the members of the congregation to pray for him as he preaches. Then he is not fighting the cold headwinds of secularism and agnosticism when he stands to speak. There is mutual striving to bring forth the word God has for his people, and to listen to it in joyous submission.

Here is what one minister told Laubach he says to his congregation: "I am very sensitive, and know whether you are praying for me. If one of you lets me down, I feel it. When you are praying for me, I feel a strange power. When *every* person in a congregation prays intensely while the pastor is preaching, a miracle happens. If it does not happen today, somebody has failed to pray. Let us make it unanimous and see what happens when *everybody* is praying."

I know what that minister was talking about, don't you? I have been in churches where I had the definite feeling that no one really wanted to be there, and that they were going to sit in judgment on every word the minister said. It was obvious that the sermon was a terrible burden he had to struggle with and then lay down. And in other churches I have felt from the moment I entered that there was a spirit of eagerness and prayerfulness there, so that the most inept minister in the world could throw away his pitiful sermon notes and open himself to the Spirit of God, trusting him to give the words that would excite the entire congregation.

In the first occasions, I have understood what it was like for Jesus to return to Nazareth and be unable to do any mighty work there because of their unbelief. And in the second I have known what it was like for Peter at Pentecost, when, even if he had been a stone, he could have opened his mouth and sung like a nightingale.

The power of God comes upon us in our praying and submitting ourselves to him, and not in any other way. That is so essential a truth, and yet we miss it as surely as if we were both blind and deaf!

In my sophisticated days after graduation from seminary, I thought the conservative and fundamentalist churches silly or hypocritical for placing so much emphasis on prayer for their revival meetings and services. Their praying is only the mouthing of clichés, I thought; they cannot or do not mean it. They ask for it only because it is a traditional part of their ecclesiastical idiom and the people expect it. It is as routine as singing a hymn before the offering or standing for the benediction at the conclusion of the service. Therefore it would be better to discontinue it altogether, and not oblige entire congregations of folk to the expression of sentiments they cannot mean or support.

But I realize more and more that such prayer is what is missing from the staidly formal services of the culturally refined churches, and that it is why even many of the preachers in these churches appear to be bored half out of their minds with the neat, clock-like precision of their orders of worship.

Having surrendered at the outset any possibility of the Spirit's interrupting the usual chain of events, they have taken the consequent second step and ceased really to believe in God at all.

They do not expect any miracles and therefore never see any. They are like children playing with a fire hose, who would be stunned with surprise if it were ever suddenly to stiffen and begin to twist this way and that, writhing under the power of the water being forced through it; they have known only a trickle, or nothing at all, for so long a time.

I remember a story from the first book I ever read on the subject of prayer, A. J. Gordon's *Quiet Talks on Prayer*. It was about an occasion when the great lay evangelist, D. L. Moody, went to preach in a church in England. There was an iciness in the congregation, and Moody could not melt it. The preacher who had stirred hundreds of thousands of people in America felt leaden and stolid as he finished his sermon. The Spirit had not moved.

All afternoon Moody dreaded going back to preach there again in the evening. It was a task he thought he could not endure.

But something happened in the evening service. It began with a look of warmth on a single face. Then it spread. Moody felt it surging like a tide, and, master preacher that he was, he rose on it, higher and higher. There was a great outpouring of Spirit, and crowds of people streamed in the aisles after the sermon.

Later, they begged Moody to stay and preach for days; they knew revival was ready to break out. But he had to go on to Scotland and promised to come back again after his meeting there.

What had happened, he wondered, to change the atmosphere in that church between the morning and evening services? When he returned from Scotland he learned the answer.

Visiting in the home of an invalid church member, Moody discovered that she had read of his work and had been praying for months that God would send him to stir the smoldering coals of heartfelt religion in her church. The morning he had preached in the church, the woman's sister had come home and mentioned that an American named Moody had been the morning speaker. Astonished, the woman had wheeled herself into her room, saying she would have no lunch. All through the afternoon and into the evening, she had struggled with God over the issue of her church's deadness and its need for a revival.

That one woman, crippled and alone, Moody was convinced, had been responsible for the dramatic change in the evening service. Singlehandedly, she had brought the Spirit into her church again.

If one person could do that, what could five do? Or ten, or a hundred?

I would not for a moment deny the importance of good preaching. It is the proclamation of the gospel in our midst that stimulates true Christian praying and keeps it on target in the first place.

But it is through prayer that the power comes to preach well, and it is through prayer that we are able to hear the preaching.

Without prayer, the best sermons sound like mere sophistry, academic voices prating of esoteric pieces of information not worth a pinch of salt to anybody, and the Christian community is not formed. Nothing galvanizes the people. Nothing comes over them like a rain of fire, and their isolation is not cured. They go out a hundred individual selves, five hundred, a thousand, and understand nothing of the meaning of "the communion of the saints."

For only God can give communion. It is not something we can work up from below. It is not something we can engineer and preach and polish into existence.

He has already given it. But we cannot appropriate it, cannot make it our own, without prayer.

Ministers ought to pray for their congregations. They are not full pastors unless they do.

One young minister said in a book recently that he honestly did not believe in prayer. He would continue to read prayers in the services, he said, because he knew some people depended on them. But he really did not have any faith in them, either for himself or for the congregation. How tragic that is, and how much the man is missing! How much his congregation is missing by not having a pastor praying for them.

Perhaps you remember Conrad Richter's portrait of a praying minister in his novel *A Simple Honorable Man*. Harry Donner, a quiet, unpretentious pastor in a small coal-mining town in Pennsylvania, is such a good man that he continually overlooks his own welfare. When a large urban church offers him a fine salary and a position of eminence, he prays about the call and decides to remain where he is because he thinks that is where God wants him to serve.

After Harry Donner dies, worn out from a life of selfless toil, his sons discuss how he used to groan at night, as if he were in great agony. One recalls the night the old man stayed with him and his wife: "It sounded like he was praying. You know how he used to break your heart sometimes when he prayed. When I was little, I never believed God could stand up to it."

Another son, determined to know more about this, calls on a woman in one of his father's former parishes, and asks her about it. She says:

"Well, you come to the right place. We heard him a couple years ago when he stayed with us on his way up to Tim's. He always liked to come here. After he went, Philip and I were talking. I told Philip it sounded to me like he was still doing in his sleep what he done all his life when he was awake, praying for them poor souls he'd seen ailing and suffering in this world. Mind you, he visited a lot of them. It sounded to me like he was eating his heart out that God didn't always answer his prayers over them. It sounded like he was begging God that this oughtn't to be and that oughtn't to be, and he had no right to let all them poor people under the harrow while folks like the Piatts rode rich and free."

That is what I meant about the congregation's missing something by not having a minister who prays.

Regardless of how fine a preacher the pastor is,
or how efficient an administrator, or how clever a
table conversationalist, he is no shepherd of Christ
if he does not pray for his congregation. No one is
more partial than I to good preaching. Yet I would
far rather have a minister who lifted me before God
than one who merely lifted me by the hair of my
head.

But if it is important that the minister pray for the
congregation, how much more important it is that
members of the congregation pray for each other. That
is part of the sadness of Richter's novel: the poor
minister is the only one praying. Somehow the congregation never learns to pray, and what little sense
of community it has centers in the figure of the pastor.

Imagine by contrast a congregation in which all the
participants are given regularly to prayer and meditation. Wouldn't you know, the moment you stepped
into its midst, you entered a matrix of warmth and
fellowship unlike any you could find in the world
outside? Wouldn't you sense the power of the group
to heal and bless, and know that the Spirit of Pentecost
was there?

A friend of mine, who has been diagnosed as having
an incurable disease, flew with her husband all the
way to Washington to worship with a congregation
which has a reputation for prayerfulness. "You could
feel something happening in the group," she said. "I
can't explain it. You have to be there to experience
it. But it's wonderful."

The friend said she was skeptical of faith healing

and wasn't looking for a miracle. "But there is a wholeness in a group of people like that," she said, "and it enters into you. You feel yourself becoming more whole. Maybe your body doesn't heal completely. I don't know about that. But your spirit discovers a new wholeness, and you know you're ready to die in a way that you weren't before."

That is the marvelous thing about the body of Christ. It is an organism, and health and power pass from one locus to another within it. Those who have been living partially receive life from those who are living more fully.

Another friend related what a friend of his had experienced in a group of praying Christians.

"We were asked to pair off and pray with the person next to us," said the friend, "while resting one hand on the other person's shoulder. It was the strangest thing. I felt as if my partner's hand were burning my shoulder as we prayed. Afterwards, I could hardly wait to get alone and pull my shirt aside to see if the flesh was really burned."

Remember Swami Rama and the heat in his palms when he meditated. Can it be that energy really does pass from person to person in a praying congregation?

The early Christians laid hands on the sick and prayed for them. Was it mere superstition that compelled them to do so? Or were they wiser than we moderns who have been inoculated with just enough knowledge of the way things work to prevent our really finding out?

John Sherrill has told in his book *They Speak in Other Tongues* how he, a sophisticated journalist, became a respectful believer in the power of a Christian congregation to achieve extraordinary results in its midst.

The analogy he used to describe his experience is memorable. He had once sung in a choir with a remarkable male singer. It had helped his own singing and he told the man so. "If you think that's something," the man had said in effect, "then next time sit right in front of me." Sherrill did. "Now lean into me as we sing," the man said. "Just put your shoulder against my chest and let's sing." The effect, said Sherrill, was unbelievable. He had never sung so well in his life.

It is a question of resonance and syntonization, in the church as in Sherrill's case. Something happens to us in a sharing, empathetic congregation. The hidden reserves of our lives are tapped. Deep flows into deep, and we experience an empowering communion.

It is no longer we who live but Christ lives in us. We become his body, in a strange, inexplicable way.

The Spirit convicts, cleanses, and heals. Our selves are transcended in a new mystical self, coextensive with all the people of God. We know a sense of community we never know any other way.

Somehow, in a mystery, the risen Christ is present in the worship, and makes himself known in ways so certain that none can doubt they have broken bread with the Master himself.

"Did not our hearts burn within us?" we echo with the disciples who traveled with him to Emmaus.

It is the risen Christ, more than anything else, that the New Testament community is all about. The church gathers around the proclamation of the kingdom and the news that the kingdom's Lord has been raised from the grave, so that he is no longer confined to a single place but can present himself to worshipers everywhere at once.

The mood of the Christian fellowship is a resur-

rection mood. It energizes us to care for others, to
hope for the redemption of the world.

And prayer which proceeds from this center, this
mood, this energy, forms a community in a way nothing else can—forms it and *re*forms it, for the community
is constantly renewed by the preaching of the resurrection and the people's response in prayer and self-
surrender.

The liturgy of the church—the worship—is a kind
of prayer the community makes in response to the
incarnation and resurrection. We may subdivide it
into hymns and prayers and versicles and offering
and communion, but in a sense it is all prayer, for
it is all what we do to commune with God, to hear
again what he has done for us and to react in thanksgiving and dedication.

Part of the time we are praying to music and part
of the time in silence; part of the time we are praying
in words and part of the time in symbolic actions;
part of the time we are praying by listening to the
Word read and preached, and part of the time by
bringing our gifts to the altar. But it is all prayer.
It is all an act of praising God, who has shown us
in Christ Jesus how he is taking our part in the world.

If liturgy becomes boring or staid or trite to people—and there is evidence to suggest that it often
does—then one of two things must be wrong. Either
those who devise liturgy, who are charged with ar-
ranging orders of service, composing public prayers,
preparing sermons and music, are missing the point
and failing to convey the sense of resurrection power
and joy the church is about; or those who attend
liturgy have come with so little preparation in private
devotions and personal dedication that they sail

through it all without ever realizing what it was about, without hearing the voice of God or recognizing the community being formed by that voice.

We have already dwelt briefly on the latter problem, in noting that there is a correlation between the fervor of private prayer and the warmth of public worship. Perhaps a word is in order about the former problem. What kinds of worship or common prayers are truly suitable vehicles for the Christian experience today?

Obviously the forms of prayer will differ from congregation to congregation. Despite the mass media, which in most respects have a homogenizing effect on the population, there is a marked pluralism of tastes and experience today. And the first rule of worship is that it should proceed from the inner personalities of the group, in the language and images which gather up the unique experiences of those gathered for praise and prayer. Otherwise it is like a plaster laid on from without, and never works deeply into the fibers of people's beings.

Worship should have a kind of group intimacy, as belonging peculiarly to the history of that group. This is not to deny the need for universality in the symbols and expressions of faith, so that the local community is aware as it worships of the communion of saints in all the world and all the ages. It is to say, though, that the universal symbols and expressions should have rootedness in the local situation. They should be immediately recognizable as having relation to the particularities of daily existence.

Within the variety of forms, however, ranging all the way from Quaker silence to high Anglicanism to multidecibel hard-rock liturgy, two things would seem to be givens.

First, the service of worship should embody enough reference to or rehearsal of the constitutive *event* of Christianity—the ministry, death, and resurrection of Jesus—to reestablish in our minds the original basis of our cult and service.

And, second, it should do so in a manner of expression and imagination sufficiently contemporary and appealing to the sensibilities to draw us into genuine prayer, into that openness of spirit in which we are again enabled to hear the voice of God speaking to us and to submit ourselves afresh to his will for our lives. If this does not happen, then we can hardly say we have worshiped.

Much has been written in recent years about the importance of human communication in worship, and how the insights of group counseling can be profitably applied within the liturgical framework. I thoroughly agree with our need to know one another in the church, to share intimacies of belief and doubt, hope and fear, care and frustration which we too seldom reveal in sacred precincts.

But it is also important to say that no amount of human interchange will ever substitute for communication with God in worship.

There is something finally depressing and demoralizing about the accumulation of human intimacy unless it is transcended by our personal will to know God and give ourselves to him. There is truth for all of us in Augustine's remark, "Our hearts are restless until they find rest in Thee." However much we feel OK, to use Thomas Harris' language, and accept others as OK, we still experience a hunger for the source of OKness, for the One who swallows up all morality and all figures of speech in an imageless mystery. We still yearn for God, for the Holy, for the Beyond and Not-yet.

Our sense of community is inseparably united to the idea of the parenthood of God, not just the brotherhood of Christ. Imagine the difference in the parable of the prodigal son if there had been no father in the story, only a brother. Even if the brother had been generous and receptive when the prodigal returned, the narrative would have been disappointing and incomplete without a father. The elder son would have had to say, "If only father had been here to see this moment!" The very existence of two sons implies a father.

It is the same with the human potential movement and the church. We need the human potential movement. We need to learn to relate to one another more freely, more honestly, more openly, more lovingly. But the church is about the divine potential movement which preceded the very notion of a human potential movement, and which laid the basis for it in the life and teachings of Jesus, who was "obedient unto the Father."

Prayer is more than self-discovery. It is self-discovery *before God.* And it is for this reason that worship is essentially prayer. It may involve visiting with a neighbor, but it is visiting with the neighbor before God. It may include the lustiness of good singing, and perhaps even dancing, but it is singing and dancing before the Lord. It may entail the deliverance of an informative or entertaining sermon, but it is a sermon heard in the presence of God.

As Kierkegaard had it in his famous image, the minister or liturgist in worship is only a prompter, a holder of cue cards, while the congregation on stage does its act before the Almighty who sits in the audience.

Or, better yet, the congregation does its act and then pauses, waiting for a word from its most important critic. It speaks and then listens, and speaks and listens again, for its transaction is finally beyond words, of the heart.

George Buttrick expressed it consummately when he said, "Corporate prayer is the heart of corporate worship. Ritual is not central; for, however necessary and vital, it is still ritual. Scripture is not central; for, however indispensable and radiant, it is still Scripture—that which is written, the record not the experience, the very word but not the Presence. Preaching is not central; for preaching, however inevitable and kindling, is still preaching—the *heralding*, not the very Lord. Friedrich Heiler has rightly written: 'Not speech *about* God but speech *to* God, not the preaching of the revelation of God, but direct intercourse with God is, strictly speaking, the worship of God.' When the rite is made central, prayer may become an incantation. When the Book is made central, prayer may become an appendage of scribal interpretations. When preaching is made central, prayer, as in even Zwingli's order of public worship, may become only an introduction and conclusion to the sermon. The heart of religion is in prayer—the uplifting of human hands, the speaking of human lips, the expectant waiting of human silence—in direct communion with the Eternal. Prayer must go *through* the rite, Scripture, symbolism, and sermon, as light through a window."

How diligent the person must be then who prepares the rite, Scripture, and sermon, that they remain transparent to the living Presence. What care must be expended in reading what is prepared, or in preaching the sermon, lest people's attention be diverted from where it should be instantly fixed when the worship is begun.

How do we dare to lead in worship, if we think about it at all? For who *can* do it, given this burden of idealism?

There is nothing that makes me tremble more, as a minister, or feel inwardly more ashamed, than the compliments paid me after a service of worship. The people mean well and wish to be polite. But how much better if they could say, "I felt the Lord today," or "I shared in the Presence."

It is time, isn't it, that we deprofessionalized the ministry, inviting more and more members of the congregation to take part in the leadership of common worship, even to the planning and delivering of the sermon, not only to renew the sense of corporate witness among the laity but to alleviate the hired minister of the terrible responsibility of standing between them and the God they are worshiping?

But whoever assumes the responsibility, Forsyth was surely right, that the best preparation for leading in common prayer is to pray. We cannot expect men and women to be converted in worship, to open themselves to the renewing power of the Holy Spirit, if we set before them forms of worship fashioned out of our unconverted imaginations. We cannot hope that they shall pray in brokenness and contrition the words of confession we assembled in a mood of hastiness and impenitence. This work is too serious for irresponsible servants. As the musician said he could tell if he had not practiced for a day and everybody could tell if he had not practiced for a week, those who worship can tell when those who lead are stiff and unaccustomed to their roles.

I have read the journal of one young minister who begins each day alone in the sanctuary of his church, singing hymns, reading prayers, and taking private communion at the table. It is filled with the excitement of these crucial moments—of the tremulous emotions, the confessed sins, the burdens of love, the joy of discipleship.

Each day a new prayer is composed and entered in the journal. Always, the prayers are the produce of meditation, of waiting before God until vision is sharpened and life is clearly focused. I have marveled at their extraordinary perceptiveness for the blessings of every day, for the richness of life when we only take the time to become attuned to it and recognize it.

One line in particular sticks in my memory, the culmination of a prayer of thanksgiving: "Bread for the wilderness, Gary, and wine for your journey."

How sensitively this young man must lead his people in their worship. How could he do otherwise, having daily prayed and worshiped thus himself? He knows when angels come and go, and fulfills the higher duty of his calling.

Perhaps some would object to the practice of taking private communion, on the grounds that it is a fellowship meal and not a Mass. But fellowship with whom? With other congregants only? Or with Christ who said, "Lo, I am with you always" and "If any person will open the door, I will come in and sup with him"?

This man understood the basis of communion, you see—the gift of God, in Christ, which binds us first of all to him as individuals and then to one another

as those who have received and recognize his grace.
It begins with each of us and God, and radiates from
there to church and world.

There is nothing symbolically more central to
prayer or to community than the table of our Lord.

This fact may elude us, for in the hustle and bustle
of modern life, and in our penchant for frozen dinners,
packaged snacks, and quick-serve hamburgers, many
of us have all but lost the memory of big family
dinners and intimate dining occasions. But the early
church never lost sight of the centrality of the meal.
Its literature was full of this.

When the story of Jesus' feeding the multitudes
in the wilderness was read in the congregations, they
understood the eucharistic significance of it. He still
fed them in the wilderness, still gave himself to them,
still formed them into a special community.

When the story of the disciples from Emmaus was
recounted, they saw the table symbolism of it. Jesus
still revealed himself to them in the breaking of bread,
and afterwards they still marveled at how their emotions kindled within them. The early church was the
Church of the Burning Heart.

When Paul wrote to the Corinthians about the supper he said, "I have only passed on to you what I
have received, that on the night when the Lord Jesus
was betrayed, he took bread and, when he had given
thanks, he broke it. . . ."

Bread for the wilderness and wine for the journey.

Whenever we worship or pray, we are table guests.
We receive what has been set before us.

Our model, in Jesus himself, is the Eucharistic
Man—the one who gives thanks and distributes what
he has.

And the miracle of it is that when we do that there is no limit to what we have. Resurrection power feeds multitudes. It heals the sick. It rejoices the broken-hearted. It claims the lonely. It shelters the homeless. It comforts the bereaved. It is, after all, the power of God, not man, and the only thing restricting it is our unbelief, our lack of faith.

When we truly enter into the spirit of the table, and become eucharistic men and women ourselves, something is unleashed in us, an energy we did not know we had. Suddenly we see all life as gift, as multisplendored opportunity. We see it, in Matthew Fox's words, as "too short to meet all the people, taste all the pleasures, love all the lovable people, witness all the world's cultures, waterfalls, and sunsets."

We become so thankful, and experience such plenitude, that we become radical donors, desirous of giving ourselves to the world in every way we can imagine. "For thanks will not be contained. Nor will it measure itself out carefully. It simply gushes over in spontaneous, free, and sometimes foolish response."

Thus the mood of the table is not dolorous and mournful, as some by their practice would represent it, but joyous and triumphal. It is not really the *Last* Supper, as we have learned to call it, but, as a friend put it in a sermon, the *First* Supper. It forever opens new doors of gratitude and perception, if we receive it prayerfully, and leads us forward into more and more fullness.

It is no wonder that Mauriac said in his old age a Low Mass quite overwhelmed him and he could no longer go to hear a High Mass every morning in the chapel on the rue de la Source as he once had done.

To the sensitive worshiper, there is finally nothing left but to utter the brief, orgiastic cry *Maranatha*—"Our Lord, come."

That—and to go.

For the community into which we are born as eucharistic men and women is a servant community, not a community of lords and ladies. Its life is in giving life, not keeping it. It perpetuates itself by refusing to close its membership, by never being satisfied until every other man and woman has become a eucharistic person too.

It follows a Lord who said, "Except a grain of corn fall into the ground and die, it abides alone."

Therefore it lives by dying, and rises by falling.

It experiences resurrection and then takes up a cross—all to teach the world to say, "*Our* Father."

It is . . . important to understand that when we come to the ultimate stage of reflection, we are back again in the world of involvement. The only way by which we can form any assessment of the person who has achieved some degree of union with God is through his attitudes towards the world and its people.

–*Douglas A. Rhymes,* Through Prayer to Reality

5

Prayer

and the World

"I am so despondent about everything," said a friend, "—crime, violence, the recession, inflation, the fuel crisis, people starving all over the world. There just doesn't seem to be any end to it. The world has never been in a bigger mess than it is right now, and things seem to be getting worse all the time."

Would it have sounded facetious if I had suggested to her that she pray for the world? Perhaps so. We are not inclined to expect much today from prayer.

There was a time when many people did have the faith to move mountains. But now, at a less figurative level, mountains are being moved all the time—rivers and lakes, houses and cities, and turnpikes, too. We are no longer impressed by mountain movers. What we need is a *world* mover. And our world is so large and complex that we despair of its ever being changed.

What if prayer only changes our attitudes toward the world, so that we are different?

That is important in itself, isn't it?

When you learn to pray meditatively, letting the right side of your brain come into its own in your life, you begin to see everything in a new way.

This in itself is extremely significant. It recovers the world for you. It brings into focus so much you were missing.

When you were a small child, everything was a miracle—the flowers on the wallpaper, the rocks in the fishbowl, the flies on the window, the stacks of colored cans at the grocery store, the postman who came to the door.

But the older you become the less you see. Your angle of vision is narrowed to shut out everything but the one object you seek. You look right past crowds of marvelous human faces to see the street sign you are searching for, or to behold some invisible pattern of thought preoccupying your mind.

Prayer does something about this.

It slows down the mental cameras, so that you view the world in slow motion. It makes you linger over details you would have missed—faces, hands, feet, bread, water, berries, blades of grass, the breeze, a scrap of melody, a thousand daily gifts.

When you pray, your heart beats slower, surer, your pulse grows steadier, your nerves relax, and awareness increases. You recover things you have lost—images of smiles, memories of words, recollections of touch, sensitivity to presence.

You become, to use McLuhan's word, an anti-environmentalist. You are rescued from your environment so that you can see it again, so that it has a reality apart from your subjugating intelligence.

Prayer revivifies the world you live in. It makes

the colors brighter, the details finer, the images sharper. It has the effect of the sun after a summer's rain: everything leaps out at you with greater clarity; with brilliance and joy.

This is especially important in connection with the people in our lives.

We are so prone, in the everydayness of things, to forget them or become insensitive to them. The closer they are to us, the truer this is. Lost in our own thoughts and labor, we respond to them as things and not as persons. We fail to listen with the inner ear, to hear what is being said behind their small talk and routine conversations. We miss the nuances of their beings, the shifting clouds and sunshine of their emotional moods.

But when you begin to pray, it is different.

Then they come alive again to you—or you come alive to them. Their hopes, joys, interests, all become palpable again. You want to respond to them with love and care, to hear their hurts and complaints, to encourage them where they doubt and falter, to praise them for things well done or said, to share their lives in a never-ending picnic. You want to be theirs, available and ready, open to meet them on their ground, not yours.

One lovely woman says that she notes a definite correspondence between her prayer life and her contact with old friends. During intensive periods of praying, she becomes concerned for persons she has not seen for months or years. Almost invariably then, she says, she receives word from them—a letter, a telephone call, a visit.

Recently she was moved to pray for a woman she had met at college four years ago. Feeling the need

to do something for the woman, though not understanding why, she also sent the woman a subscription
to a particular religious journal.

Shortly afterwards, the woman wrote to say, "You
always seem to know the right thing to do at the
right time." The woman's husband had died and an
article in the magazine had given her unusual comfort.

"I knew nothing of her husband's death until she
wrote," said the first woman. "She took it for granted
that I knew."

Howard Thurman, the noted black preacher, has
written of a similar sensitivity in his own prayer life.
A member of his church in California had become
incurably ill. Each day he stopped by to read or pray
with her. When he had to make a trip east, he gave
her a table of the time changes along his route, so
that they could continue to pray at the same time
each day.

One morning as he knelt to pray, he received a
definite impression that the woman had died. A telephone call verified his feeling.

Their praying had established such a rapport between them that they were as present to one another
as if they had been in the same room.

I have noticed that during certain periods of my
own prayer life when I am feeling empathetic with
certain persons and their problems I will hear, almost
uncannily, from other persons with similar problems.
Sensitivity appears to beget sensitivity.

Earlier this year, for example, I was concerned about
a friend whose son had leukemia. Then I became
acquainted with a woman whose son was dying of
another type of cancer. I was praying daily for both
of these persons and their sons.

Then one morning the phone rang as we were having breakfast. The male voice on the other end of the line was choked with weeping.

"John, pray for me," I heard.

I did not recognize the voice and asked whose it was. It was a man I had not seen for three years, with whom I had had a business association six years ago.

His son had committed suicide three days before. He and his wife and other child were leaving immediately on a trip to try to assimilate their tragedy.

I was flying to Texas that day on a speaking trip. For a week I not only prayed for my two friends whose sons were facing death but prayed every few minutes for this man and his family in their terrible numbness.

But why had he called me instead of the minister who conducted his son's funeral? I had never been related to him as a minister, and had not seen him for years. I had no special reputation for piety. Was it because I was praying for persons who faced the loss of their sons?

In Texas, I preached in the church of a minister whose daughter had died of leukemia three years earlier. I talked with him and his wife about their experience of loss, and prayed for them as I prayed for my other friends.

The minister was in the process of publishing a book about his daughter's death. In the publisher's office, I secured the galley proofs and carried them home with me on the plane.

The evening I arrived home we went to dinner with the woman whose son had cancer, and I gave her the galleys to read.

While we were dining, the woman who prepared

the meals at the restaurant learned that I was a writer and asked if she might talk with me.

I followed her into a little glassed-in room adjacent to the kitchen. It contained a child's bed and toys. It had been her son's playroom, she explained. Her son was a retarded child. For seventeen years he had stayed in that room where she could watch over him as she worked. At night she had slept with her hand on his body, ready to respond to his need in any emergency. She loved him dearly, almost indescribably.

And he had died only a few months ago.

She handed me an account of his life which she had written. She wanted me to read it and see if I thought it publishable. It it were, she said, she would like to use the royalties to establish a fund for other retarded children.

There was another person to add to my prayers.

It is impossible for me to explain this unusual convergence of grieving parents on my consciousness all at the same time. Did it just happen, for no particular reason? Perhaps so. But I am inclined to think it was more than that.

I believe it was a matter of sensitivity at the time— that my concern for one person and then another became a psychological magnet drawing the others with similar problems. It seemed to me that it was my mission during that period to pray for persons experiencing a special kind of loss.

If I had missed the first or second one, I doubt if I should ever have known of the others. It was a cumulative thing.

There is something about prayer, about letting the mind be still and waiting upon God, that sensitizes us to the world around us—to the glory of sunsets and the beauty of tears.

Thomas Merton describes it in this passage from *Contemplative Prayer:*

"This is an age that, by its very nature as a time of crisis, of revolution, of struggle, calls for the special searching and questioning which are the work of the monk in his meditation and prayer. For the monk searches not only his own heart: he plunges deep into the heart of that world of which he remains a part although he seems to have 'left' it. In reality the monk abandons the world only in order to listen more intently to the deepest and most neglected voices that proceed from its inner depth."

Listening to those voices does change you—profoundly.

You want to redesign the world in such a way that people are made to suffer less. You want the hungry to be fed and the infirm to walk. You want the blind to see and the deaf to hear. You want parents to love their children and children to grow up happy and morally committed to the right things.

You yourself become committed to the kingdom man has always dreamed of.

As Isaiah in the temple became aware of the need for a spokesman for God and said, "Here am I, send me," you find yourself ready to help with the kingdom.

As Peter at prayer on a rooftop had a vision symbolizing the Gentile nations and the next morning set out for Joppa in the company of a Gentile officer, you discover an eagerness in yourself to help the people you once considered unworthy of assistance.

As Paul in his prayers saw a man of Macedonia

saying, "Come over and help us," and went, you awaken to the deep desire for your vision of life to become more than a vision, to become a reality, and suddenly you are committing yourself to a tide which will carry you to a whole new personality and a whole new style of living.

Even your enemies cease to be your enemies.

I saw this dramatically through the diary of a student friend whom I shall call Sloan.

Sloan bitterly disliked a young man who had taken his place in a rooming house where Sloan lived before he was married. He was very fond of the elderly woman who managed the house, and was obviously jealous of the attentions she now lavished on the new boarder.

The boy was probably on drugs, wrote Sloan, because he remained in bed most of the day and did almost nothing to assist the old woman. When he, Sloan, had lived there, he had helped with household chores and had mowed the grass.

A bit later in the diary, the suspicions had become confirmed. The boy had been arrested for possession of heroin.

Sloan was angry. The woman had paid the boy's bail. Clearly the boy was no good, and the woman could not afford to spend her money on him that way!

But then something happened in Sloan's life. He became ashamed of his attitude and began to pray for the boy.

It was discovered that the boy was ill, and after his trial he was sent to a detention hospital.

The more Sloan prayed for him, the more concerned

he became. He began to visit the boy in the hospital
and to pray for his rehabilitation. The old hatred
ceased to appear in the journal entries. Instead there
was loving concern. The person he had regarded as
an enemy had become a friend.

As Thomas Kelly said in *A Testament of Devotion*,
two things happen at once when we pray: we become
detached from the world *(contemptus mundi)* and we
become committed to it *(amor mundi)*.

"He plucks the world out of our hearts, loosening
the chains of attachment. And He hurls the world
into our hearts, where we and He together carry it
in infinitely tender love."

We pray for our friends, we pray for our enemies,
we pray for people halfway around the world whom
we have never even seen. The world matters to us
in a new way.

But let us grant that we are changed when we pray,
and that prayer thereby makes a difference in the
world. The question remains, Can prayer really change
the world? Does it have an objective validity quite
apart from the psychological alterations in the life of
the person praying?

How you answer will depend on your appraisal of
how the world and the universe are constituted.

As I indicated earlier, my own attitude has changed
considerably in recent years. My eyes have been
opened to the deeper mystery of things. I have much
less regard for my own limited rational and scientific
view of how things happen, and much more respect
for the transcendent and miraculous aspects of existence.

A friend recently told me this story. He had pulled

his car to a stop at an intersection when he suddenly heard the sounds of grinding metal and breaking glass. Looking around, he saw no source for the sounds. He realized the noise was a terrible premonition.

The light was changing, and he knew he must prevent the car in the lane beside him from proceeding. Looking over, he managed to get the other driver's attention and divert him momentarily.

Then, without even sounding its horn, another vehicle came hurtling through the intersection at top speed—without stopping for the red light.

"When the car was gone," said my friend, "the noise stopped, and I engaged the gears and drove on."

He had narrowly averted disaster—and for a reason that would never fit into a naturalistic view of the world.

Remember the story of Olive I told in chapter one? I repeated that story during a sermon.

Afterwards, a woman came up to me and said, "I have a story I'd like to share with you."

Her father, she said, was a very religious person and almost always attended church. One Sunday morning, however, he said that he felt like going for a drive instead of going to church.

Driving along a small state road, he noticed a dirt road entering the woods. Overwhelmed with a desire to follow it, he turned off the road and did so.

Presently he came upon a pickup truck, and could see that there was a man sitting in it. Thinking the man might be having some kind of trouble, he stopped his car and walked up to the window of the truck.

"Is anything wrong?" he asked.

"Yes, there is," said the man. "I'm dying."

The man had been deer hunting and had accidentally shot himself in the leg. An artery was gushing blood. He had managed to drag himself back to the truck, but was too weak to drive.

After a tourniquet had been applied to his leg and he had been taken safely to the hospital, the man said, "I prayed and prayed for somebody to come and help me, but I figured it was no use, because nobody ever uses that old road."

I can't dismiss stories like that. After a while, they accumulate to the point where you cannot take them lightly.

One night I had dinner with Dr. Glenn Olds, president of Kent State University, and heard him tell about having Uri Geller as a dinner guest a few evenings before then.

Geller is the young Israeli with a remarkable reputation for all kinds of psychic abilities. I had recently read two extensive articles about him in a prominent intellectual magazine, and was especially fascinated by his reported ability to bend keys and rings and table utensils merely by concentrating on them.

Scientists from Stanford University had been dumbfounded at his "tricks," and had been unable to discern any evidence whatsoever of deceit or fraud in his performance.

"After our meal," said Dr. Olds, "my wife could hardly wait to lay a spoon in the center of the table and ask Mr. Geller to bend it. He said he would see if he could. He passed his hand over it a few times, and when I looked it appeared to be bent. I thought it must be an optical illusion. He continued to concentrate on it, though, and before he had finished it was clearly bent out of shape."

The maid, who had witnessed this from the doorway, said Dr. Olds, produced an old spoon from the kitchen and asked if Mr. Geller would bend it so she could take it home and show her children.

Again he concentrated, and again the spoon gradually left its original shape.

One of the table guests, a scientist from the university, excused himself and returned to the party some fifteen minutes later. He had hurried home, he explained, to fetch a metal object he was pretty sure Mr. Geller could not bend. It was a heavy medal which he had won in World War II, and it was shaped like a cross.

As the professor held the cross in his hand, said Dr. Olds, the tips of it began perceptibly to incline upwards—more and more—until the medal looked like a flower.

"That scientist went home," said Dr. Olds, "shaking his head and saying he would have to reexamine all his assumptions."

One of the greatest scientists of our time, Albert Einstein, was convinced that matter and spirit are much more intimately interrelated than our common sense tells us they are.

It is entirely possible, he said, if all the conditions in the universe were precisely right at a given moment—conjunctions of the planets, incidence of the sun, alignment of atoms, harmony of the mind—that a person could pass his or her hand cleanly through the other hand, as though it were spectral instead of material.

What are we to make of the amazing story of "Arigo," the commonly educated Brazilian social worker who baffled the medical doctors of three continents with his ability to perform highly complex diagnoses and operations while "inhabited" by the soul of a German doctor who died in 1918, the year he was born?

The doctors who visited Arigo's rough "clinic" could not believe their eyes when they saw the miracles he did every day, writing elaborate prescriptions though he had not had a day of training in pharmacology and removing cataracts and tumors though he had never had any instruction in surgery. The incisions he made barely bled, as though the flesh were welded or glued back together the moment he touched it.

Most of the patients did not even lie down for their operations, and they appeared to feel absolutely no pain.

One doctor, Dr. Henry Andrija K. Puharich, a graduate of Northwestern University, submitted to the removal of a tumor on his arm in order to experience Arigo's treatment firsthand and to have it photographed with movie equipment for further study. Within five seconds, Arigo had removed the tumor and plopped it into his hand. Dr. Puharich had not even felt the incision, and it bled only the faintest trace of blood.

According to John G. Fuller, the journalist who has written a book about Arigo, the humble man began his healing sessions each day by repeating the Lord's Prayer. During the prayer, he would begin to take on a definite German accent in his speech, though he had never studied German or been exposed to it. From then on, he moved and spoke as a man possessed.

A team of doctors who set up a clinic of their own to check Arigo's diagnoses found that in 545 cases his diagnoses agreed with theirs 518 times.

I have never seen Arigo. He is now dead, from a

car accident in 1972. How do I know he wasn't a fraud?

I never saw Leonardo da Vinci. How do I know the stories of his genius are not mere fiction?

I have never seen an atom. How can I be sure the physicists aren't pulling my leg?

I have never seen a viral bacillus. How do I know for sure that viruses are not caused by fires on the moon or by crabs in the ocean?

There are many things I can never know, but must receive in faith. I do not want to be stupidly credulous, accepting every fairy tale as if it were fact and every miraculous occurrence as if it were an incontrovertible datum. But neither do I want to draw my world too small, foreclosing possibilities that some future physics may underwrite as empirically true.

Once in my life I made the mistake of assuming that human science had already taken all the essential measurements of life on our planet, and that all that remained was to clear up some relatively small areas of mystery.

Now I see that the whole universe has *Mystery* written across it, and that our marvelous systems themselves are never any better or surer than the hypotheses on which they were originally predicated.

It is time we went back and listened again to *old* wisdom, reassessing our Hobbesian or Cartesian world-view and fitting it into patterns that are larger than it is. Until we do, we are behaving like immature children who have learned a few new facts about life and think that the whole can be fitted into those.

I confess I do not know the absolute limits of our power in prayer. But I am convinced they are considerably beyond what we presently estimate them to be.

Take the matter of prayer and healing, for example. We know so little about the world of the body. A hundred years from now, our present medical practice may seem largely barbaric and primitive. Diseases and conditions now considered submissive only to strong drugs and operations may then respond far more favorably to biofeedback methods, psychic surgery, or prayer.

As one outstanding internist confessed to me, "Our knowledge of these things is like a tiny bonfire lit on the forward edge of a dark, sprawling continent. There is so much to learn!"

There are very few doctors, he said, who don't believe in prayer for their patients.

I had a woman student who in her forties received a theological degree and became a minister. In one of her first charges, a woman asked her to visit the woman's elderly mother, who was dying and in a semi-coma.

"She is very religious," the woman explained as she showed the minister into the darkened room where her mother lay. "She would appreciate it if you would pray with her."

The minister entered alone and sat quietly by the bedside a few minutes, listening to the irregular breathing. Before leaving, she stood over the woman and prayed for her.

The next morning, the daughter phoned in a state of excitement. "I don't know what you did to mama," she said, "but she's all right this morning! She wants to get out of bed."

"Actually," the minister told me, "I prayed for God to ease her body and make her comfortable. I asked for his will to be done in her. I did not specifically ask for her to be made well again."

But the woman did recover sufficiently to live a fairly normal life for several more months.

What accounts for such miracles? Would the woman have recovered anyway? Or did the minister's words touch some hidden spring in her psyche, releasing pent-up energy her body needed to make her well? Or did God somehow use the minister to transmit power to the woman that was not already resident in her body?

Prayer is opening ourselves to God
so that he can open us to others.

—Louis Evely
Our Prayer

We are often baffled today by reports of renewed efforts among certain church groups to recover the power of healing the sick. This is especially true when the reports concern traditionally intellectual churches such as the Presbyterian and Episcopalian.

How many of the healings are true healings and how many involve psycho-suggestion? Are there certain illnesses which are amenable to prayer and suggestion, and others which cannot be touched by faith at all? I do not know what to say, except that I am reverent of most claims until I see definite evidence that fraud or hypocrisy is involved.

While I was writing earlier parts of this book, my own mother entered the hospital for an operation for cancer. Seventeen years earlier she had had a mastectomy of the left breast. Now an ominous shadow the size of a golfball had appeared on the x-rays of her left lung.

By what seemed almost a miraculous coincidence in itself, we were with her when she received the report of the shadow. My wife and I had been in Washington, D.C., and decided on an impulse to drive two hundred miles out of our way and go by my parents' home as we returned. We hadn't been there in six months. But we were there the one morning when we were able to lend encouragement as the report arrived.

As mother made her preparations for the hospital, we hurried home and readied things to return and be with her during the operation. Friends on every hand promised to pray for her. An entire faculty of nuns at the convent school where our sons receive piano instruction said prayers for her each day.

The operation was performed. The doctors scratched their heads. They had been certain, they said, it was a tumor. They ran tests.

Days later, they decided it must have been a scar produced by an attack of pleurisy. They were not sure. But they couldn't get over the fact that it was not a tumor.

Could prayer possibly have made such a difference as this? It seems unlikely, but I do not know. Stranger things have happened.

I know I am responsive to something John Yungblut has written about intercession in his little book *Rediscovering Prayer*. He says he knows that when he prays for the sick or dying something happens to him that is good.

But more than that, he says, "I believe something else is happening, less obvious but nonetheless real. I believe my prayer works both *for* God and *for* this person. It *does* something. I don't want to try to say what it does, because I don't understand it. And anyway it seems to me important that I not fix in my mind anything I would acknowledge as an answer to my prayer. As I must commit into God's keeping my friend and his condition, I must commit into his keeping my own partial and blundering efforts on his behalf. But I do feel confident that, in a world in which physical energies like light, sound, color, and electrical charges can move invisibly and interconnect matter in space, spiritual energies must also interconnect and interpenetrate in some way as yet unknown. Therefore, in my prayer for my friend I provide God an additional channel for the movement of his energies to my friend. I believe my prayer on his behalf does something good for my friend, whether he recovers or dies."

If the parapsychologists are convincing in their evidence that people's minds can control the rolling of dice, then surely there are spiritual energies which can heal and bless. If there is indeed a power like Uri Geller's capable of distorting metal objects without visible force, then surely we cannot scoff at what religious people for centuries have called the power of prayer.

There was a time, in the superstitious infancy of the human race, when it was necessary to become skeptical in order to learn more about nature and its inherent miracles. Now perhaps we live in an opposite time, when, most people having become skeptical through scientific teaching, it is important to suspend our disbelief in order to learn even more.

It is amazing how miraculous daily events may seem to be when you are open to the possibility that they are affected by prayer. During a recent prayer seminar, for example, a woman well disciplined in prayer revealed one day that since the beginning of the seminar she had made a habit of praying each week for the two persons sitting beside her during the previous session. As there were no assigned seats in the seminar, and the chairs were always arranged in a circle, she had normally been seated by different persons each week. The week before, she had been seated between a forty-year-old minister and myself.

Immediately our minds raced back across the week.

I recalled the extraordinary day I had experienced on Monday. It had been a busy season, with many out-of-town engagements, consultations with several doctoral students, and the usual pressures of lectures and seminary classes. I had been caught up in the routineness of it all, unable to relax, living in daily fatigue.

But Monday I had decided to take the day off. My wife and I wandered through stores, ate a leisurely lunch at a little restaurant she had wanted me to visit, and took a long walk in the afternoon, holding hands and talking.

It was one of those lovely spontaneous days you don't plan but follow, the way a child follows a butterfly. I don't know when I have had such a refreshing time. The most remarkable part was the way I had dropped so easily out of gear.

I wondered—was it because I was being prayed for?

The minister too was astonished.

He had had a most unusual week. He had had an article accepted by a national magazine, had received the proofs on a new book he had written, and was called to a new church.

He had needed a week like that, he said. A couple

of years earlier he had been asked to resign from a southern church because of his sympathies with blacks, and he had returned to the seminary for doctoral work and some healing time. But apparently the dismissal from a church had dogged his path as he talked to several pulpit committees during the past year, for none had proceeded beyond the early stages of negotiations to call him. Now everything had come in a bunch the week he was being prayed for.

Maybe all these things were coincidental, but neither he nor I felt that they were. To us, they had an aura of the miraculous about them.

Frank Laubach said that he cultivated the practice of saying quick little prayers for people he passed on the street or sat near on public conveyances. He would bring his whole self into the prayer, he said, as though his very body and nervous system were beaming it toward the person. Almost invariably, it seemed, if the person was not occupied with reading or talking to someone else, he or she would look around at Laubach and make some comment about religion.

He said this practice was like a tonic to him when he was tired. Somehow it always gave him a lift, as if an extra measure of energy had been injected into him.

Shortly after reading Laubach's little book *Prayer: The Mightiest Force in the World,* I was in another city to preach at a church there. I was staying in a private club where most of the residents were elderly men.

On Sunday morning there were only three guests in the rooftop restaurant for breakfast—two men who appeared to be in their nineties, and me. It was so quiet I could hear their labored breathing, could hear their dentures clicking, could hear their coffee cups clatter on the saucers as they attempted to set them down.

For some reason, the usual waiter had not appeared for work, and a young woman who did not normally work at that hour was serving breakfast. One of the old men was terribly upset that the regular waiter was not there and that he must recite for this strange woman his order for breakfast.

"No, no," he cried as she started to pour him a cup of coffee, "I never drink coffee. I drink hot chocolate. Where is my waiter? What are you doing here? He knows what I want for breakfast."

Restraining tears, the young woman returned to the kitchen.

How awful it must be, I thought, to live with yourself when you are that miserable.

Then I thought of Laubach's practice of beaming prayers at the back of people's heads. Would it work? I wouldn't know if I didn't try.

"God," I said, "he can't stand himself. Please make the day a little easier for him. Let him find some softness in his heart."

In a moment the young woman returned to wait on the other old man. As she passed the table of the one I had just prayed for, he reached out to stop her.

"I'm sorry, my dear," he said. "I don't know what came over me. That was very rude of me. I hope I didn't hurt your feelings."

I had the same feeling I had when I was seven, aimed a gun at a bird, pulled the trigger, and watched the bird fall.

I couldn't believe it had happened.

But it had.

These are mainly evidences only for faith, not for unfaith. They will not convince anyone who is not already convinced.

But suppose there is something to them, and that our prayers for others do make a difference, even when they do not know we are praying for them. What a difference we could make for the kingdom of God by spending time in intercession for others.

Laubach, who did so much for the peoples of Africa and Asia, was completely convinced of the importance of such prayer.

We should pray for people as we read the newspaper and listen to the radio, he said. Learn to say a ten-second prayer for this person and that person all through the day. Pray for the leaders of the world, he said—for the President of the United States, the Prime Minister of England, the rulers of Russia and China, and all others whose decisions affect the destinies of so many.

What would happen to our world if ten million people prayed daily for these persons? Ten million people, all praying for God's will to be done through our leaders, all helping to move mankind closer to the kingdom.

What if ten million people earnestly committed themselves to pray for food for the starving tribes of Africa? Half of them might pray for the United Nations and the World Bank to lend assistance, and the other half might pray for the national leaders in Africa, that they would arrange delivery of provisions with less pilferage and profiteering.

Surely something would happen if all that creative energy were directed toward the same goal.

Is it a bad time for prayer? Many people plead that

they are too busy, though they wish they could do better. They don't seem to give prayer a very high priority rating in their lives.

Perhaps we should ponder again the old story of "The Nun of Lyons," which Buttrick retold in his Cole Lectures on the eve of the Second World War.

She was dancing at a fashionable ball, and was far and away the most radiant girl on the floor, for her engagement to the most eligible bachelor in the city had just been announced.

Suddenly she stopped, for she saw a vision!

It was the world dying for the lack of prayer.

She gasped at the sight.

When she looked back at the dance, she gasped at that too, for now it had the appearance of a *danse macabre,* a dance of death. Her eye caught a priest in the corner chatting with a mother about the marriageable girls—even the church did not know that the world was dying for want of prayer.

Her vow was instantaneous: she must spend her life praying for the world! Nothing could dissuade her. She founded a contemplative order and spent the rest of her life praying—lest the world die.

Is it such a far-fetched tale?

I remember a dear old lady I used to visit once a week during a pastorate in New England. She had come to this country half a century earlier as a midwife, and had delivered over five thousand babies since her arrival.

Now she was an invalid confined to a corner bedroom in the upstairs of her son's home. She sat all day in a wheelchair, and when her son came home from work in the evenings he moved her to the bed. She had grown so heavy with a great tumor hanging at her side that he was the only one strong enough to move her.

But for all her discomfort she was a lovely, quick-witted woman, and I never came from her room without feeling more joyful than I had been when I entered.

Often, when I went, I would find her sitting near the window, where she could watch the small children playing in a field nearby.

"I am praying for them" she told me. "Every day I pray for them. I am not good for anything else, God knows, but I pray that they will grow up healthy and good. It is what I can do for them."

Mother Crossley has been dead for several years now. But I sometimes think of her and wish that my children had someone looking over them the very same way. Imagine how wonderful it would be to have a remarkable woman like that praying for you, and not even to know it!

"It is what I can do for them."

It is what we can all do.

And it is what the world needs.

If only there were a window like hers looking out on all the children of the world. Or ten thousand windows like hers. Or ten thousand *times* ten thousand.

It would be an entirely different world tomorrow.

That kind of praying is not mere wishful thinking. It is real prayer. It is lending your own powers of concentration and desire to God for his use in the world.

It harmonizes with the yearning of his own heart for the kingdom, for the day when all people will live in wonderful peace, with each one offering himself or herself in love and gentleness to all the others.

It expresses again for our time the dream of Jesus and the early Christians for the reign of God on earth, dispelling sin and suffering the way the first rays of the morning sun dispel the darkness.

If only my friend who felt despondent because the world is in such great confusion could have sat for a little while with Mother Crossley, and seen the world from her window, how different it all might have seemed to her.

She might still have seen the turmoil.

But she would have known what she could do about it.

About the author:

John Killinger is professor of preaching, worship, and literature at Vanderbilt University Divinity School. He received the S.T.B. in theology from Harvard Divinity School, the Ph.D. in English from the University of Kentucky, and the Th.D. in homiletics from Princeton. Dr. Killinger has had a broad background as a pastor, academic dean, and professor of English, as well as theologian. He is author of more than twenty books, and has recently been at work on a novel. He and his wife, Anne, collaborate on music, and have done a musical comedy, several hymns, and a musical for children. The Killingers have traveled extensively, and have lived in Paris and England.

ALSO BY JOHN KILLINGER

All You Lonely People/ All You Lovely People
(#80315). How often do you admit your loneliness or
find escape from its crippling frustration? Killinger
recalls meetings, incidents, confrontations, and emotions to demonstrate how people can share each
other's lives. He brings you insights into the very
essence of sharing relationships.

For God's Sake, Be Human (QP #2814-1). A warmly
personal account of the religious experience that
makes sense. A well-written bridge between 'old-time
religion' and modern sensibilities.

WORD BOOKS FOR
FURTHER READING

Prayers for Worship by E. Lee Phillips (#0137-5).
Worship, as we can all testify, can easily slip into a rut.
Here is help for the minister, the worship leader, and
the congregation seeking richness and dimension in
public worship. More than 200 prayers in 8 helpful
sections.

Lord, Let Them Know I Care by William H. Fields
(#2854-0). A collection of prayers and meditations
from the life of a minister seeking to receive from God,
and then share with others, strength, wisdom, and
hope in the daily sorrows and joys of human existence.

Two-Way Prayer by Priscilla Brandt (#0022-0). It's
one thing to learn how to pray to God; it's quite another
to learn how to listen for answers. Two-Way Prayer
opens a whole new world of spiritual growth. Priscilla
Brandt shows us how to experience the reality of
Two-Way Prayer, and tells us how it has changed her
own life and the lives of thousands she has taught.

How to Be the Lord's Prayer by Norman K. Elliot (#2851-6). An exercise in entering the mind of Jesus—seeing life through His eyes, making decisions by His scale of values, and finding God in the light of His experience. "Here, at last, is a book that interprets the Lord's Prayer as the Lord himself intended us to interpret it."—Dr. Frank C. Laubach.

Care and Maintenance for the Christian Life by William L. Blevins (#0139-1). Answers basic, recurring questions which speak to the new Christian and also to the Christian who feels the need for a fresh start. Blevins helps the new believer better understand the direction of the pilgrimage with Christ. And he supplies more mature Christians with the basic skills to renew spiritual life on the verge of going stale.

The Seven Deadly Virtues by Gerald Mann (#2853-2). "Evil attacks the Christian, not at his weak points, but at his strong." Often, in our sincere zeal to do good and see evil eradicated, we unconsciously fall into one or more of the Seven Deadly Virtues: Censoriousness—The Virtue of God's Gestapo; Permissiveness—The Virtue of the Free-Loader; Childishness—The Virtue of the Serviceless Servant; Exhibitionism—The Virtue of the Holy Hawker; Certitude—The Virtue of Secondhand Faith; Velvet Violence—The Virtue of the Righteously Indignant; Independence—The Virtue of the Irresponsible. A study of the ethics of Christ for mature Christians.